Contribute: Hassle-Free Content Control

Bill Barrett

Marc A. Garrett

Michael D. Hazard

Brandon Heffernan

Lyn Wall

Published by glasshaus Ltd,
Arden House,
1102 Warwick Road,
Acocks Green,
Birmingham,
B27 6BH, UK

ISBN 978-1-59059-177-2

Contribute: Hassle-Free Content Control

labor-saving devices for web professionals

Trademark Acknowledgments

Credits

Authors
Bill Barrett
Marc A. Garrett
Michael D. Hazard
Brandon Heffernan
Lyn Wall

Technical Reviewers
Dave Addey
Bill Barrett
Tony Ford
Marc A. Garrett
Mid Jamie
Bob Regan
Michael Walston
Ray West

Proof Reader
Agnes Wiggers

Communications Manager
Bruce Lawson

Commissioning Editor
Amanda Kay

Technical Editors
Matt Machell
Chris Mills

Publisher
Viv Emery

Project Manager
Beckie Stones

Production Coordinator
Rachel Taylor

Cover
Dawn Chellingworth

Indexer
Bill Johncocks

Cover Image

The cover image of this book was created by Don Synstelien of *http://www.synfonts.com*, co-author of the glasshaus book *Usability: The Site Speaks For Itself* (ISBN: 1904151-03-5). You can find more of Don's illustration work online at *http://www.synstelien.com*.

About the Authors

Bill Barrett

Bill Barrett is a web designer based in New York. In addition to current freelance projects under the aegis of Web Five Design, he has worked for several years at a dot-com-era web design boutique in SoHo and currently is the Senior Web Producer at Antigenics, a biotech company based in the Rockefeller Center working to cure cancer. As part of an in-house communications and design team, he provides strategic direction and manages all web design and development projects. He is also an Oberlin Conservatory-trained classical musician (organist), has studied social ethics and religion during several years at Union Theological Seminary, and loves heated political debate. He lives in Queens with his boyfriend of five years, Cenon.

Marc A. Garrett

Marc A. Garrett, a Macromedia Associate Partner, is a developer based in New York. For the last five years Marc has run *since1968.com*, featuring conversations with industry leaders in web design and development. Today Marc does freelance database and web application development.

Marc earned a BA in English from the University of Georgia and a JD from American University. He has worked with clients in the United States, Europe, and Asia. He is partial to funny hats.

Michael D. Hazard

Acknowledgements: Thanks to my beautiful wife Laurie, who put up with my strange work hours and constant pacing, all while being pregnant with our first child. Now that the book is finished, we'll have more time for each other. Thanks also go to my parents who stuck with me as I meandered my way through college. Thanks for never giving up hope that one day I'd graduate. It was your support that got me through.

I'd also like to recognize the people I've worked with over the years. In your own way, each of you has contributed something to this book.

Brandon Heffernan

Brandon is a technical writer and instructional designer who lives in upstate New York. He has written several instructor-led training courses on web technologies and software, including Cascading Style Sheets, web design and usability, ColdFusion, HTML, Dreamweaver, and many others. Brandon is also an online instructor for a variety of web design and development courses through Barnes & Noble University and Element K. This sort of stuff occupies about a third of his life. His other interests include "finishing" his so-called novel, cartooning, books, films, and golf (without apology). He realizes that many of these interests are short-bio clichés, but hey!

Brandon would like to thank his trusty coffee maker, Mike Hazard, and the clever folks at Titleist.

Lyn Wall

Lyn Wall is a freelance web developer. She received her BA from Cornell University and MBA from SUNY Albany. She has worked in many industries, including retail, personnel, and antiques. After several years working in the IT department at a large Oil & Gas company, Lyn left to pursue opportunities as an MS Access contractor. She got her start in web development designing and creating a site for her family business and has developed and promoted several other sites.

Lyn lives with her daughter and four cats in Houston, Texas.

Table of Contents

Introduction

As a web professional, you have probably found yourself in a number of situations where you had to rely on one or more content contributors to provide the content for a web site you were developing.

Isn't it an annoying waste of time when your content contributors constantly hassle you to make changes to their content? They haven't got the technical expertise to go into your web pages and make the changes themselves without breaking your code, so all the work of amending content goes to you.

You have probably wished many times that there was a way to allow them access to just the content on the site so they can make their own changes, without having to shell out for an expensive content management system. Your content contributors probably feel the same way: they don't want to waste time asking you for changes that they could easily make themselves, and you can often become a bottleneck for their work when they depend on you for changes.

Well, a solution has arrived, in the form of **Macromedia Contribute**, a web content editing tool that empowers content contributors to edit their content to their heart's content without any danger of breaking the web site, while allowing you, the web professional, to retain overall control. It's easy to install, easy to use, and – at $99 per user license – it's inexpensive.

Who's this Book for?

This book is for any web professional who wants to give their content contributors access to their material so they can edit it whenever necessary, without having to waste the web professional's time, and without fear of breaking the web site.

It teaches you every discipline necessary to implement and support a successful Contribute system, from convincing your boss that it's worth investing some time and money in, to implementing the system, giving your users access to the pages they need to edit, customizing the interface, using Dreamweaver templates, training your users, supporting the system after implementation, and much more.

In addition, we have provided an **End-User Training Guide**, which can be downloaded free of charge at *http://www.glasshaus.com*. You should download this and give a copy to everyone who will be using your Contribute implementation to edit web site content. It contains everything your Contribute users will need to know.

What do I Need to Begin?

To start developing a Contribute system using this book you only really need a single copy of Contribute (either a full version, or the trial version from *http://www.macromedia.com/software/contribute/trial/*) and a suitable server to host the web sites you will access through Contribute.

However, in a production environment, you will need a full copy of Contribute for each user who is going to be editing Contribute content. We also recommend that you obtain a copy of Dreamweaver MX. (If you already have this, we suggest getting hold of the newest point release, 6.1, which has in-built Contribute functionality and can be updated to at *http://www.macromedia.com/software/dreamweaver/special/updater/*). You don't need Dreamweaver MX to use Contribute, but it makes it a lot easier in several ways, for example, when you want to create templates to enable and control your users' creation of new pages.

In addition, you will need to download further software for use with *Chapter 8*, which looks at using Contribute to update dynamic web sites; this will depend on which server-side language you intend to use to develop dynamic web sites. You can find more specific details in the chapter and its code download.

Also, there's an example web site called *Our Company,* which we'll be using to demonstrate techniques and examples in some of the chapters. This is downloadable from *http://www.glasshaus.com*, along with all the other sample code.

Finally, as mentioned above, there's the End-User Training Guide that you can distribute to your users.

What's Inside?

This book comprises the following 8 chapters:

- *Chapter 1* provides a quick introduction to the world of Contribute – what is it, why is it useful, and what are its advantages and limitations?

- In *Chapter 2* we get our hands dirty looking at how to set up and administer Contribute. This includes getting your users connected to your web site through Contribute, security, and looking at some important Contribute features such as Rollbacks and Check In/Check Out

- *Chapter 3* covers the usage of some of the more advanced web page editing features offered by Contribute such as working with images and hyperlinks, and adding MS Word documents and Excel spreadsheets to pages

- In *Chapter 4* we look at how we can customize Contribute to better suit your own needs, by providing a custom Welcome page, modifying the How Do I... panel, adding custom user groups, and setting Contribute Preferences...

- *Chapter 5* looks at how we can enforce best practices and uphold standards amongst our Contribute users: both our own style conventions and coding standards, and globally recognized standards, such as Web Accessibility

- Next we turn to *Chapter 6* for a look at Soft Skills – how can we convince our boss and our users that adopting Contribute is a great idea, and how best to go about training our users to use Contribute, and providing support for it after implementation?

- *Chapter 7* looks at using Dreamweaver templates with Contribute – how to build a good template, and how to set up Contribute so that our users can only access the templates they need to work with

- In *Chapter 8* we look at how Contribute can be effectively used to update content on dynamic web sites, through clever use of server-side includes

Support/Feedback

Although we aim for perfection, the sad fact of book publication is that a few errors will slip through. We would like to apologize for any errors that have reached this book despite our efforts. If you spot such an error, please let us know about it using the e-mail address support@glasshaus.com. If it's something that will help other readers then we'll put it up on the errata page at *http://www.glasshaus.com*.

This address can also be used to access our support network. If you have trouble running any of the code in this book, or have a related question that you feel the book didn't answer, please e-mail your problem to the above address quoting the title of the book, the last 4 digits of the ISBN for this book (1280), and the chapter and page number of your query.

In addition, the example code for this and every other glasshaus book can be downloaded from our web site.

1

In this Chapter

- Why is Contribute useful?

- Overview of Contribute's main features and capabilities

- Contribute's advantages and limitations

Author: Bill Barrett

An Introduction to Contribute

Contribute allows web developers to maintain the control they need over a web site, while offering content editors the freedom to make changes to web content without assistance. It automates many tasks that a small-organization web developer would normally perform, and then extends those capabilities to others who know very little or nothing about web development.

Designed to capitalize on the widespread knowledge of word processing skills, Contribute is more like a word processor than an HTML-authoring application – users can style text, add graphics, and add links with the use of a simple toolbar. Contribute also takes away the hassle of shuttling multiple files back and forth between a local drive and the web server. It is designed with a unique "browse-and-edit" interface (much like a browser) so that all the editing takes place in a single, simple, unified console.

Contribute is available from Macromedia at http://www.macromedia.com/software/contribute/ (you can download a trial version for free, or the full version for $99).

Contribute allows web developers to maintain the control they need over a web site, while offering content editors the freedom to make changes to web content without assistance

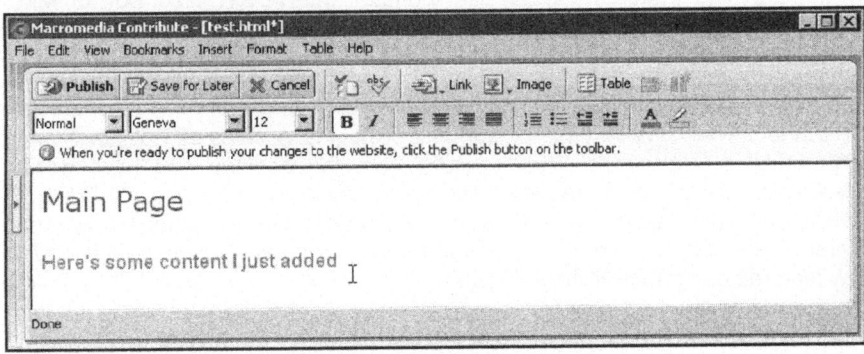

The Contribute editing interface.

Contribute can save web developers, especially those who work with independent content editors/providers, hours of time, since the majority of edits tend to involve minor textual alterations that someone else can now quite easily perform, saving both the developer and the person wanting the change made time, hassle, and frustration.

For example, consider the following scenario:

Arianne works for a small company that develops medical web sites for physicians. On one site she maintains, she works with an off-site editor who compiles and edits content written by academic physicians on the advisory board. The task of maintaining the web site falls on two people: Arianne, the web developer, and Robert, the editor.

In a typical week, Arianne receives a lot of content to put up on the site – she converts it from MS Word to HTML, puts it up on the password-protected server, then sends Robert a mail asking him to check out the URLs, and give approval/submit changes.

A day or two later, Arianne receives Robert's reply e-mail, to which is attached a new Microsoft Word file. This document contains a list of small changes he wants her to make to the pages: swap two paragraphs; bold that phrase; omit this word; move that image to the other side of the page, etc. Each web page has a list of changes that Arianne diligently performs. After completing all the changes, she re-uploads the pages to the server, sends another e-mail to Robert, and awaits his second (and hopefully final) review.

What typically happens now is that Robert sends her another e-mail requesting changes, which annoys Arianne, as she has to interrupt other work to go back and make them, then send Robert another request for approval. Robert feels guilty about sending these mails, as he knows that the changes he requested are small and annoying, and wishes he were simply able to make those corrections himself.

This process could be repeated 3 or 4 times before approval is made – it is easy to see how much time and hassle could be saved if Robert were able to make the changes himself using Contribute.

What Are the Alternatives?

Until now, small organizations have had few options for editing and managing their content. Enterprise content management systems (CMSs) like Vignette, Interwoven, Red Dot, or Microsoft Content Management Server, because of their extremely high costs and complex configurations, are clearly out of the price range – and out of scope – for small and even some medium-sized organizations. Their cost is almost always over $100,000 and implementation can take it into the millions.

There are other low-end content management applications, such as eZ Publish Desktop Edition, that are very similar to Contribute. They operate from the desktop and have word-processor-like interfaces, while connecting to the web server via standard web protocols like FTP, WebDAV, or XML-PRC. Contribute fits into this category more neatly than any other (as we shall see in more detail later, Contribute is NOT a fully-fledged CMS), though it does give a nod to some other workflow features of the more robust CMSs.

Apart from specific content management software solutions, developers and their content contributors can also use professional-level HTML-authoring applications that incorporate some kind of site-level management to satisfy their content management and workflow needs. Dreamweaver MX and Adobe GoLive, for instance, allow for workgroup configurations with collaboration tools that check in and check out files as they are edited. The disadvantages of this method are that each user must tackle the learning curve of the professional web development application, and could conceivably modify every aspect of a page, providing little control for the developer over what happens with the pages on the site. These professional tools cost around $300 per user to implement, which is still a lot more than Contribute.

Finally, some brave developers have adopted home-made solutions for basic content management of their sites. These typically use simple Perl, PHP, or ASP scripts that process form input from a web form. This method can get the job done effectively and with practically no cost other than labor from the developer. However, it is by far the least flexible or robust option.

So, there are other options but, especially for small to medium-sized companies, Contribute is the most sensible option, providing all the features needed for content editors to edit their content, while allowing the developer to maintain control over the integrity of the site, all in a low-cost, easy-to-implement package.

Contribute's Main Features

In this section we will go through Contribute's main features.

No Server Software

Contribute is a desktop application for computers running Microsoft Windows or Mac OS X. The software comprises two elements: a browsing engine based on Internet Explorer and the HTML-authoring engine of Dreamweaver MX. Contribute communicates with web sites on any server through the use of FTP or a local area network (LAN) connection. Contribute requires no server-side components installed on the web server, only needing to store a few utility files in common file formats to handle things like administrative settings, access logs, and versions of pages that can be used to roll back changes.

User Privileges and Administrative Settings

Contribute can dole out user privileges as necessary. Different user groups with different editing privileges can be created for editing specifically assigned areas of a site. Content editors then install Contribute on their PCs and gain their privileges by receiving a connection key (a special file from the administrator) with an encrypted password. Users never see the FTP or LAN settings. Once users click on the connection key and enter their assigned password successfully, they can start editing pages. This provides a convenient layer of security to your web site: if you ever need to decommission a user (assuming you have set up individual users) or a group of users, that person or group can't reconnect to the site later on. *Chapter 2* goes into detail about setting up users and user groups.

The administrator also has the responsibility of creating a set of privileges for each user group that is created. This is probably the most important part of setting up Contribute. Contribute provides a fairly wide range of editing capabilities, from locking down all objects on a page except text, to full editing of objects on the page (including links, images, and tables), as well as adding or deleting pages. Depending on how these settings are chosen, your Contribute users can be limited strictly to textual edits, or they can be allowed to have significant control over design elements. By design, Contribute does not display to a user any dynamically-generated markup, such as content from a database. There is a setting, however, that specifically protects non-HTML code from being modified by Contribute. These two features effectively lock down all dynamic code so that it remains untouched by the user and by Contribute.

It's worth noting that although it's helpful for a web developer to be familiar with all of Contribute's capabilities, it is not actually necessary to own a copy of Contribute to administer a Contribute-compatible web site. A web site can be administered through Contribute *or* Dreamweaver MX (earlier versions of Dreamweaver MX need the free updater for Contribute, available from *http://www.macromedia.com/support/contribute/*).

Macromedia's strategy is to position Contribute as a tool primarily for content contributors, while Dreamweaver MX is reserved for seasoned web developers and site administrators. Of course, if you plan to administer a Contribute site and train your users, I highly recommend familiarizing yourself both with Contribute's editing features and how it handles code behind the scenes. The chapters that follow aim to help you do just that.

Ease-of-use, Workflow, and Templates

The ease-of-use of Contribute's editing interface is one of its strongest features. Editing your page is as easy as using a simple word processor, whether an edit involves only adding and styling text, or everything from adding links and images to adding/deleting table columns or rows. The more added flexibility you offer your users, the more you will have to concentrate on dealing with possible inconsistencies in fonts, styles, colors, or markup changes.

If you do not plan to limit users to text-only editing or employ templates with locked regions, you will need to familiarize yourself as much as possible with how Contribute will affect your pages. Though the easy Word-like interface is very intuitive and simple for most users, it can potentially cause more clean-up work for the web developers ultimately responsible for those pages. This book will help you through the questions and problems you will encounter.

Among Contribute's features for end users is its very handy workflow feature that streamlines the review process for new or edited pages. Unpublished drafts can be saved and reviewed with Contribute. With a single command, Contribute will conveniently generate a "please review" e-mail with a direct link to the draft page. This provides a significant advantage over some online browser-based forms of content management that don't offer this capability. See the *Contribute as a Content Management Tool* section later in this chapter for more on how Contribute's features compare to other content management tools.

Contribute also offers a rollback capability that saves up to 99 earlier versions (!) of each page in case the need arises to revert to previous content. This is a notable feature, especially if your users are working directly on the production server of your web site, which will probably be the case in most Contribute workflows.

Contribute has several methods of dealing with templates, something you'll no doubt end up taking advantage of. You can create new templates in Dreamweaver with locked regions, create a template by hand, or (allow your users to) use one of a variety of pre-defined templates provided by Contribute. You can also allow users to start with a completely blank page or (better yet) create new pages based on existing pages on your site. See *Chapter 7* for more about using templates with Contribute.

Contribute's Target Audience

Contribute is designed to specifically meet the needs of web developers and content contributors in small to medium-sized organizations. There are a number of groups that Contribute will be widely used and appreciated by:

- Small organizations or businesses where budgets and resources are limited
- Non-profit organizations who cannot afford to hire a web professional
- Freelance developers who want to empower their clients to make changes or to perform basic maintenance on their content
- Educational institutions where teachers or students will be creating and maintaining individual web sites for their classes, personal interests, or assignments

Although Contribute could and probably will be used with some effectiveness in larger organizations, it is much more suited to organizations or situations where there are one or more experienced web developers and a handful of content contributors, and where workflow complications are limited.

Benefits and Limitations of Using Contribute

Now we have seen the most important features of Contribute, let's have a look at its benefits and limitations.

Benefits

Macromedia specifically bills Contribute as a new class of software that meets the needs of business users who don't know HTML or anything about web development. Contribute has a number of advantages in organizations where one developer is the sole conduit for all web development and maintenance. Contribute can benefit these organizations in the following ways:

- **Quick and easy set-up**: An administrator can set up a site in several minutes, and a contributor can begin editing immediately. There are no server installations or configuration files to worry about – just install the desktop application and create the site settings and user privileges
- **Short learning curve**: A content contributor can learn to use most features of Contribute in minutes without any special knowledge or training (they don't even need to know HTML, although HTML knowledge is useful for dealing with images and links)
- **Low cost**: Contribute's low cost ($99) allows it to be deployed in many business or education environments. New users can be added with little effort or cost, and Macromedia offers discounts for bulk buying licenses

- **Empowers content contributors:** Contribute finally unleashes the web content author or contributor from relying on a web developer's time and skills to make simple changes to the web site, which causes frustration, and can result in bottlenecks. Most content additions and page editing can be handled without the involvement of the web developer, allowing changes to be made more conveniently and efficiently

- **Eases strain on developers**: Contribute eliminates the need for web developers to get too involved in content maintenance and lets them focus on development projects

- **Good dynamic code protection:** Web developers are rightly concerned about the impact Contribute users without HTML/coding experience may have on their code. Contribute minimizes major disruptions to the code and keeps all functionality intact, as it mostly only allows textual content to be changed, rather than the markup that surrounds it

- **Unique support options**: Macromedia hosts an excellent (and free) forum for users to post questions and delve for answers on their web site at *http://webforums.macromedia.com/contribute/*. In addition to Macromedia's regular support center, the community forum is an excellent and up-to-date place to learn about the application. The forum is often visited by Macromedia product managers and support staff. As a developer, you can also fully customize Contribute's help pages, as you will see in *Chapter 4*

Limitations

Contribute also has some shortcomings that could limit its usefulness and potential if you were not aware of them:

- **Limited control over code-writing practices**: Contribute provides very limited control over how sourcecode is written. This has been an ongoing problem with WYSIWIG authoring applications from their first appearance on the market. The problem has been largely solved in the enterprise authoring applications by providing the developer with a method to control how sourcecode is written, by establishing their own markup layout rules. It is disappointing that Contribute does not provide this control as well. This would be an important way to assure developers that the integrity of their code will be respected, even when Contribute needs to rewrite some of it during an editing session

- **Minimal site-level awareness**: Contribute does a fine job of maintaining intra-site link integrity and ensuring that the URLs for embedded objects are valid, but its site awareness stops there. For instance, for a developer who may maintain mirror copies of a site, Contribute lacks the capability to create a site-wide report of all activity by Contribute users. Logs are maintained in each individual directory, but this is not very useful to developers trying to open up the site for contributors while maintaining some level of oversight and monitoring

- **Mediocre support for accessibility and web standards**: In addition to the disconcerting fact that Contribute does not by default write XHTML or (at the very least) HTML 4-compliant code (it defaults to deprecated fonts and alignment markup practices), the software also doesn't support as many accessibility options as it could. For instance, while the alt image attribute is available for a user to complete, and can also be enforced by the site settings, the "title" attribute (used within almost any HTML tag, but most often the `<a>` tag) is conspicuously missing. It seems at least as important as alt attributes, but cannot be implemented in Contribute at all

- **Security**: For the many web developers who already use standard FTP to transfer their web pages and assets to the web server, Contribute presents no problem. For those developers who deal with sensitive data or are more security-conscious, however, there is currently no support for SFTP or other secure protocols to transfer web assets. Contribute can certainly be used behind a firewall with LAN or FTP, but it can't be used as it was intended to: interacting with a production server. Macromedia representatives have said security features are in the works, but until then web developers with demanding security requirements may be forced to avoid using Contribute

Contribute's Capabilities

With the exception of the administrative setting that will be managed by the developer, Contribute's features can be divided into two broad categories: **web page authoring/editing capabilities** and **content management capabilities**. In order to see on how Contribute can meet the basic authoring and content management needs of small organizations, and for developers to decide whether it is the right solution for their particular development and content challenges, we can evaluate how Contribute fits in to the overall picture by comparing its capabilities to those of other commonly used applications that it aims to replace or integrate with.

Contribute As an HTML Editor

Contribute is not a full-fledged HTML-authoring application, and so can't really be used as a replacement for Dreamweaver, unless you are only dealing with the most simple of web sites. Macromedia has chosen to include only the most important content manipulation facilities, which they think the users will need to make changes to the pages. Below is a review of important capabilities that Contribute has successfully implemented.

- **Editing web page content**: Contribute's prime strength that it allows anyone to easily edit content in existing web pages. Its "browse-and-edit" feature is unique and is the most convenient interface for making small, quick edits. Users of Dreamweaver MX, on the other hand, would first have to identify a file by name, download the file, and then edit the code in Code or Design view. Contribute's word-processor-like interface is well suited for business users who have never worked with HTML, whereas advanced HTML-authoring applications with multiple palettes and options can confuse non-technical users

- **Creating or deleting web pages**: Contribute's solid support for templates allows users to easily add new pages, though template creation itself is best left to Dreamweaver MX. Contribute can create templates from existing pages and also create completely blank new pages (very common tasks), but most templates cannot be created or edited in Contribute. Contribute users, if given proper privileges by the administrator, can also delete pages one at a time

- **Managing styles:** Contribute provides some flexibility for applying styles to text and objects, using either `<font>` elements or standard CSS class rules (both of which mimic MS Word's style selection icons). Both these methods can be turned on and off by the administrator to maintain control over the coding of stylistic elements. Stylesheets cannot be created, edited, or viewed in Contribute – this is left to the developer

- **Handling links, images, and other functionality:** Adding, editing, or deleting functional objects such as links or images is fairly simple in Contribute, but you can't manipulate advanced objects such as linked pop-up windows or image rollovers. Contribute protects the novice contributor from breaking links and images by integrating a link checker that runs before publishing a page, as does Dreamweaver MX. Both Contribute and other authoring applications provide solid support for putting Microsoft Word or Excel content into a web page. While Contribute's *import* features are slicker than those of other applications, its *translation* of the content such as character entities into HTML is not as robust, and needs more work by Macromedia to become fool-proof (for more details, see *Chapter 3*)

The table below summarizes the different features available in Contribute and Dreamweaver, and which application provides which. This allows you to see what can be handled by Contribute users, and what needs to be left to those with access to Dreamweaver MX (more likely to be the developer):

Feature	Contribute	Dreamweaver MX
"Browse-and-edit"	✔	
No knowledge of HTML needed	✔	
Low cost	✔	
Short learning curve	✔	
Add links and images	✔	✔
Add Flash objects	✔	✔
Easily add Microsoft Word and Excel content	✔	✔
Good HTML translation of MS Word and Excel content		✔
Apply styles to text and objects	✔	✔
Create/edit stylesheets		✔
Maintain local copy of site		✔
Site management tools		✔
Create and edit dynamic content		✔
Use templates	✔	✔
Create/edit templates		✔
Editable regions/locked code	✔	✔
Integration with other web development applications		✔
Sourcecode editing		✔

Contribute As a Content Management Tool

Just as Contribute is not a fully-fledged HTML-authoring application, it is not a fully-fledged content management solution either. Contribute does incorporate some basic content management capabilities that could be found in any low-end content management system, but Macromedia coolly rolled them (and simplified them) into a workable and inexpensive solution for small-organization web developers and content contributors. Let's take a look at what content management capabilities Contribute delivers to its users:

- **Solid usability:** Macromedia has made it ridiculously simple for a contributor to interface with the web server, and Contribute's simple user interface solidly establishes it as a user-friendly way for contributors to add and edit content on a web site

- **Versioning**: Contribute offers single-page rollback of up to 99 previous versions. Limiting the application to single-page rollbacks seems reasonable given Contribute's target audience, in comparison to the ability of larger CMSs to roll back to a previous version of an entire site. Contribute is geared toward a single user (or a few users) and their workflow, whereas an average fully-fledged CMS manages a much larger, more complex operation

- **Managing concurrent changes**: Contribute provides a standard check in/check out feature as all CMSs do, and prevents concurrent editing by locking a file once it is in use. Contribute rightly avoids the complex and sticky issues of parallel development and page reconciliation that larger organizations may need in a CMS

- **Enforced workflow**: The only workflow feature that Contribute includes is an "e-mail review," which automates the task of sending a temporary link to someone in an e-mail, so they can review the new or edited page. This is a convenient feature, but it does not enforce a review before publishing, something that web developers have often wished for. It automates this common task for the user, but does not add an extra layer of workflow by reserving the publishing function for more privileged users as enterprise-level CMSs do

- **Staging and Deployment**: The larger a publishing group gets, the more staging and approval is necessary before new content can be deployed. Contribute however is squarely meant for small publishing teams where deployment happens instantaneously on the production server, after an optional staging and informal review of draft pages. In slightly larger publishing groups, it is possible that Contribute may be used differently: it might interface only with a development (staging) server, and content could be deployed manually by an authorized person (using an FTP application rather than Contribute, for example) after all edits have been completed by Contribute users on the staging server. However Contribute is ultimately used, its primary focus is a small-organization approach to staging and deployment, that is, in all likelihood the person editing the content will be the one who publishes it to the live site. When the needs of an organization using Contribute outgrow this reality, the organization will have to think about adopting another, more robust CMS solution

- **Managing web assets**: Contribute does not manage web assets as many CMSs and document management applications do. Since Contribute is desktop-based and operates in tandem with a single web server at a time, it only has the ability to upload to the server those assets from local drives that are used or linked to in the edited web pages. Contribute does allow access to all assets stored on the server, but should an asset on the server be changed, replaced, or deleted, there will inevitably be an incorrect asset or broken link on the site, at least until the next edit of a page containing that asset

- **Templating**: Employing templates is perhaps Contribute's strongest selling point and is the heart of any content management solution, providing a much-needed separation of presentation (design) from content. Multiple templates can be made available to the user and can provide an endless variety of options for creating new pages in a site. Templates, as would be expected, cannot be edited by the user but, if given appropriate privileges, the user can create a new page that is based on an existing page, a flexibility that Contribute users are almost sure to need. Templating doesn't only serve end-users well: developers have just as much to gain from a well-implemented templating system. One of the most important needs of a developer is to lock global, infrequently updated sections of pages to maintain consistency across a site. Dreamweaver MX's "locked regions" (areas of the page template that are uneditable by users) form the heart of Contribute's templating system

Code Versus Content: The Struggle Continues

Contribute is the place where the interests of web developers and content contributors intersect. Contribute was designed with the flexibility to allow a problem manager to find a solution to meet the needs of both web developers and content contributors, two groups that are sometimes at odds.

Web developers are concerned with clean code, structured markup, elegant design, and technically sound and accessible web pages. Content contributors (designers, copy editors, and other asset creators) are more concerned with being able to edit web content easily and quickly without having to ask developers to make changes or being concerned with the code behind the content. The ongoing struggle of "code versus content", or as it manifests in this case, "web developer versus content contributor", will continue long into the future. Contribute forces web developers and content contributors to try to understand each other better and provides a solution that will hopefully please both sides.

> *Contribute was designed with the flexibility to allow a problem manager to find a solution to meet the needs of both web developers and content contributors, two groups that are sometimes at odds.*

Articulating Web Developers' Concerns

Web developers have been waiting for a tool to come along that will help relieve the inconvenience and time drain of endless update requests from zealous, but well-intentioned content editors. In the past, the small-organization web developer has been forced to act as the intermediary between the content editor and their associated web pages. This technology gap – properly marking up content and publishing it to the web server – has caused much frustration among web developers and editors. Developers would be happy to see this gap bridged by content editors, and to remove themselves from everyday publishing tasks that they see as menial.

Web developers have also been fiercely eager to protect the markup, programming code, and designs they've worked so hard to produce. Developers avoid tools that modify page markup and leave them few options to control how that markup is coded. They also reject applications that rewrite code in ways that essentially "break" its functionality or ruin the markup syntax. Web developers are also wary of relinquishing too much control over site architecture and design elements, which could cause disarray and inconsistency if pages are added or styles changed willy-nilly. Having the ability to apply a different visual identity at a later time requires that CSS styles be employed without exception and that they be applied consistently across an entire site. Contribute can help developers address these needs if it is configured properly.

Finally, many web developers are strongly committed to web standards-compliance and the full accessibility of their code. Tools that do not take these concerns seriously are gradually losing their credibility among web developers. Developers are rightly wary of relinquishing control of their pages and relegating their sourcecode to untrained people and outdated or inadequate software that does not meet their explicit requirements.

Understanding Content Contributors

The main problem amongst content contributors has always been that they are reliant on the expertise of web developers, even for changes that take only a few minutes or several seconds; therefore, they are subject to the time constraints and schedule of web developers.

Their one wish has always been to be able to easily edit content without coming up against the bottleneck of the web developer. It would also be a significant plus for them to be able to create and stage their own new content pages, especially when this content does not require advanced markup or programming. Since many content editors use standard word processing and spreadsheet software such as Microsoft Office, they would like to see an easy way to format their content into HTML, without worrying about how the content will be "translated" by the web developer who may not understand fully what the writer/editor was trying to achieve. Their content often needs to be edited again after they see it in HTML.

Content contributors are also better qualified to review and maintain content to keep it up to date, accurate, and relevant. It is much easier to directly edit content on the web page than it is to make a list and describe each change to someone else – then have to review the edits again after they have been made. Content contributors in small organizations have been yearning for a way to streamline their content management by limiting their reliance on the web developer. Content editors (and their managers alike) will be very happy to have an inexpensive tool that is both effortless to learn and empowers them to really "own" their content.

Summary

In this chapter we have:

- Introduced you to Contribute
- Taken a 10,000-foot view of its features and functionality
- Looked at the problems that exist between web developers and content editors, and how Contribute aims to solve these problems

The best thing about Contribute is that it is able to pull together so many important issues among web developers and content contributors into an application that is a cinch to use. While Contribute is intentionally limited in its scope, it does have a remarkable set of capabilities that begin to address a very urgent need in the small-business community: making a web site accessible to the people that need to work on it, yet protecting it from technical mistakes and code destruction that have occurred in the past when non-technical users have attempted to edit web content.

Contribute is the application that will begin to free web developers from the mundane tasks of content management, while empowering content contributors to gain a level of access to their content that they have only imagined before. This book will help you discover the possibilities and realities that Contribute has now boldly proclaimed. Read on...

2

In this Chapter

- Overview of Contribute administration

- Web site structure design

- Creating an administrator account

- Administering a site

Author: Michael D. Hazard

Site Definitions and Connections

Before content developers start using Contribute to create and update pages on a site, you need to set up site definitions and connections. You can use either Contribute or Dreamweaver MX to set up and manage your sites. Whether you use Contribute or Dreamweaver MX, the process is the same. To create a connection to a site and manage groups, you will need to:

- Set network and web server permissions
- Set up your web site's folder structure so it is suitable for Contribute
- Use the connection wizard to create an administrator account for your web site
- Create new Contribute groups and set their permissions
- create a connection key for the group
- Distribute the connection key to your users

In this chapter we'll start with a general overview of Contribute administrative concepts such as **permission groups** and **connection keys**, then move on to a detailed hands-on explanation. Next we'll learn how they are used to classify users and manage web sites. Furthermore, you will discover ways to set up your web sites so that they fit the Contribute model.

An Overview of Contribute Administration

The Contribute model consists of an **administrator** who manages site access, and **users** who develop and update content. Each user is a member of a group, called a **permission group** that the administrator creates and sets permissions for. This model is designed for a collaborative environment, where numerous users create and edit web site content. Contribute handles not only the HTML code generation, but also user access to files on the web server.

Permission Groups

Permission groups are used to define the level of access Contribute users have to assets on your web site. When you create a permission group, you define what folders the group has permission to edit, and the type of underlying code that Contribute will generate when a group is editing a page. You can also associate site templates with individual permission groups. Permission groups are more than a simple way of restricting access to files – they dictate how content developers use Contribute. Depending on which settings you select when creating a permission group, the Contribute interface, and the HTML code it generates, will change.

The Windows version of Contribute uses the Internet Explorer code base for browsing pages, while the Macintosh version uses a modified version of the Opera browser. In Edit mode, Contribute uses a scaled-down, modified version of the Dreamweaver MX IDE. It is important to test your templates in Contribute's Edit mode because pages may look different in Contribute compared to Dreamweaver MX.

What permission groups are and how they affect the way Contribute works is completely hidden from your end users. If you associate templates with a user group, only those templates are displayed when a member of the permission group creates a new page, even if the site itself contains dozens of other templates. The only time a Contribute user is aware of the restrictions you've placed on their ability to modify pages is when they browse and attempt to edit pages they don't have permission to edit.

Contribute employs a full web browser; therefore users can browse any site on the Web using Contribute. They can even use Contribute to submit forms. When browsing a site that they supply content for, they are able to browse any page on the site, even those that they do not have permission to edit. If they browse a page they do not have permission to edit, Contribute displays a message under the address bar stating they do not have permission to edit the page, as seen below.

Since the page is part of the site they are responsible for, this may be confusing to Contribute users, who are typically not tech-savvy. It is important that, when training your users, you make sure they understand that they will only be allowed to edit pages that they are responsible for. This is especially important because, as the web professional administering the site, your e-mail address is displayed in the message, and you want to avoid unnecessary support e-mails.

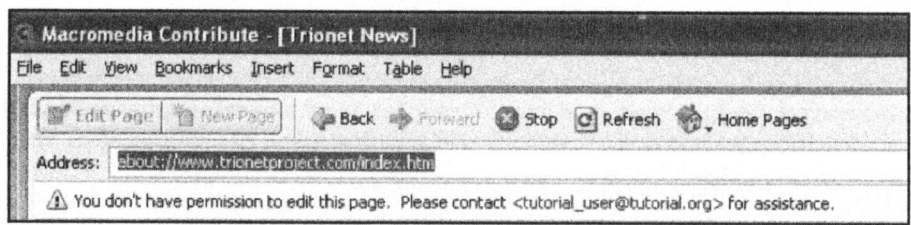

How Contribute informs a user they don't have editing permissions.

Connection Keys

Once a permission group is created, and the rules governing the group are set, the administrator can generate a **connection key**. This contains all of the information needed to connect a user to the web site. Once the connection key is created, it is sent via e-mail to members of the permission group or placed on a shared network drive. Users in the permission group who receive the file simply open it, supply a password, and Contribute automatically connects them to the site.

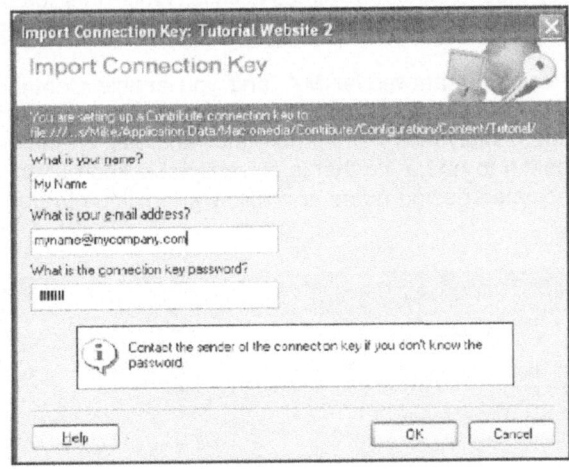

The connection key dialog

When a user double-clicks a connection key, they are prompted to supply their name, e-mail address, and the connection key password. As the administrator, you set the password for the connection key. Users should have no problem locating a connection key because connection key files use the .stc file extension and have their own unique icon.

A connection key removes the need to send sensitive information such as FTP account login passwords to end users. Since Contribute reads the file and creates the connection based on the information it finds in the connection key, important information is never exposed to your users. What's more, since Contribute creates the connection, you reduce the number of hours you spend supporting connection problems.

*SECURITY NOTE: The password you assign to a connection key is not the same password used to connect to the network or FTP server. The connection key password is used only by Contribute to verify that the user has permission to open the connection key file. It is highly recommended that you **do not** use the same password for your connection key as you do for your network or FTP login.*

Connection keys are encrypted using 128-bit encryption, and are therefore very difficult to crack. You should feel reasonably comfortable mailing connection keys to your end users. If you have concerns, consider delivering connection keys another way or setting up each Contribute user in person. The connection key is not required to set up a user; it's there only to make setup easier.

Check In/Check Out

Contribute is designed to work within a collaborative environment, where multiple users create and update files. In such an environment, it would be possible for more than one user to edit a single file at the same time, and in doing so, overwrite the other's work. In order to avoid this, Contribute and Dreamweaver MX contain **Check In/Check Out** features. If enabled, a file being edited by a user is checked out, and cannot be modified by another user. The file is essentially locked to Dreamweaver and Contribute users, though not from direct access. While this feature is optional when using Dreamweaver MX alone, it must be turned on for Contribute-enabled sites.

If you set up a site using Dreamweaver MX, and you enable Contribute, Dreamweaver MX will automatically enable Check In/Check Out. This functionality requires that all users, administrators and content developers, supply their name and e-mail address. This information is supplied to other users who are attempting to edit a file that is currently checked out. In addition, the information is used in the file's associated design notes and rollback functions to denote who checked a file out and when.

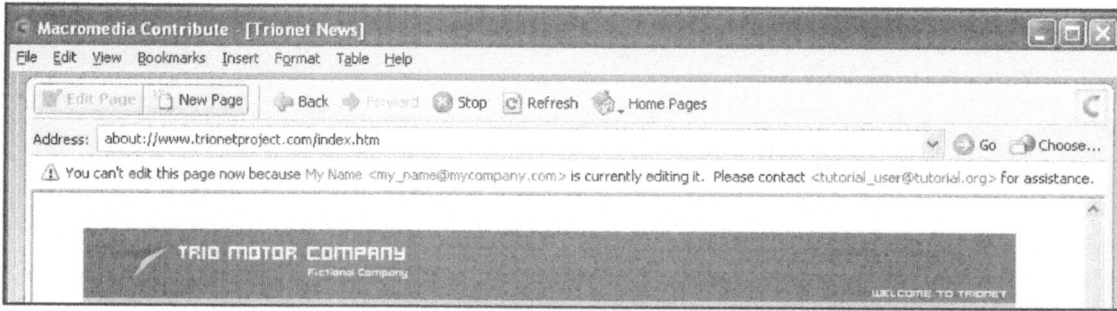

How Contribute warns of a checked out file

If a user is editing a file, it is locked. A second user cannot edit the file until the first publishes it. The name and e-mail address of the user currently editing the file is displayed below the address bar. Users can click on the e-mail address and send a message to the user listed, requesting the file be published. The web site administrator e-mail address is also displayed. Keep this in mind. As the site administrator, your e-mail address is always available to Contribute users. It's important that you train Contribute users adequately or they will use that e-mail address often!

Dreamweaver does not lock a file by setting file properties through the web server file system. Instead, it creates a .lck file that denotes that the file is locked. It is possible to override a locked, checked-out file in Dreamweaver MX. It is not possible to do this in Contribute. If your organization uses both Contribute and Dreamweaver, it is recommended that Dreamweaver users do not override checked-out files. If a file is checked out by a Contribute user and the Contribute user saves the page for later, the file remains checked out in his/her name. If a Dreamweaver user overrides the check out, changes the page, and checks it back in, the Contribute user will not see these changes when he/she returns to the draft because drafts are saved with a temporary filename. Therefore, if the Contribute user publishes their file, they overwrite the Dreamweaver user's changes. This can cause a lot of confusion.

Rollback

Contribute allows you to store previous versions of your published pages and restore them as needed. For example, if a user updates a page, a copy of the original page, without the updates, is stored on the web server. If, at a later date, a user wants to return the page to the state it existed prior to the changes, they can use the **rollback** feature.

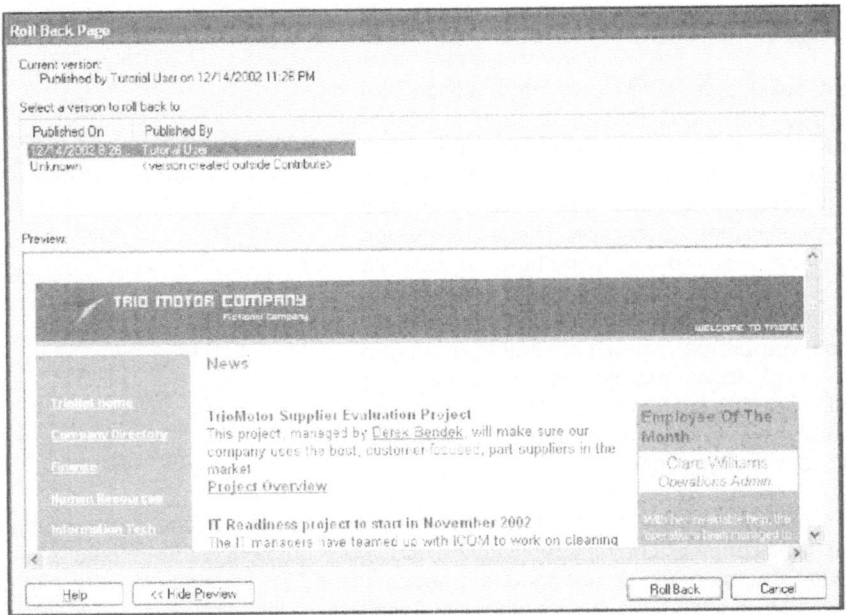

The Roll Back Page window

The *Roll Back Page* window displays information about the history of the page. It lists the date the current version was published as well as the name of the user who published it. It also lists the previous versions of the page and a preview of the previous version.

Only site administrators can enable the rollback feature, but any user can roll back a page. When a user chooses *File > Rollback to Previous Version,* the previous versions of the page are listed in the *Roll Back Page* window, and the date the page was published and the user who published it is listed in the top pane. Clicking on the page displays a preview in the bottom pane of the window. If a page was edited outside of Contribute, no information is given in the top pane, but the page can still be restored.

Rollback versions of pages are stored in the _baks folder on the web site. Pages are given the .bak extension, although the content of the file is the HTML code of the original file. The _notes folder stores information relating to the history of the file. Administrators can set the number of rollbacks to be saved through the Contribute administration tools. The maximum number of rollbacks that can be stored is 99.

It is important to remember that a copy of the entire page is saved when rollback is enabled. Storing 99 copies of a single file can consume a lot of space on your server's hard drive. If your site is large, changes often, and space is limited on your web server, you may want to consider reducing the number of versions to save or not enabling the feature. If disabled, the *Rollback To Previous Version* option in the *File* menu is dimmed for all users of the site.

Folder and File Permissions

Content developers within your organization can access your site with Contribute through an FTP or a Local/Network connection. Whichever connection method you choose, you must make sure that the account used for updates has read, write, and modify permissions to the site. These permission settings are required for Contribute to operate correctly, but are not controlled within Contribute. If you experience problems connecting to a site the first time you create a new connection, then you should check these permissions. Refer to your network operating system documentation for more information on setting them and, if necessary, consult your IT department.

Contribute permissions are separate from FTP and LAN permissions. FTP and LAN permissions relate to your network or FTP server software, and cannot be modified through Contribute. If you or your users experience problems connecting to a site, and a permission problem is suspected, you must change the permissions within your FTP server software or your network administration software.

If you're using FTP, your users will need permission to delete, overwrite, and rename. By default, some of these permissions may be disabled and you should enable them before you begin creating groups in Contribute. You do not need to create multiple FTP accounts to work with Contribute. One account is acceptable because you can use Contribute to lock groups of users into specific folders. Just remember that the one account must have delete, overwrite, and rename permission.

Security

When you enable a site to work with Contribute, the application creates several folders that store Contribute-related information. For example, the folder _mm contains connection information for permission groups. The connection information is stored in an XML file called contribute.xml. The contribute.xml file, also known as the **shared web site administration settings file** or **shared settings file**, contains sensitive information about connections to your web site. Any sensitive information in this file, such as passwords and e-mail addresses, is encrypted using 128-bit encryption, so it is safe. However, as a security precaution you should also ensure that folders whose names begin with an underscore cannot be browsed. While the sensitive information is encrypted, you do not want visitors to your site to be able to download or view this file.

`contribute.xml` *in Dreamweaver*

It is beyond the scope of this book to discuss web server configuration, and since there are so many web server software packages available, it would be impossible to discuss them all. However, it is extremely important that you ensure that your site is properly configured to block users from browsing folders starting with an underscore. Most Microsoft IIS web servers do not allow visitors to browse a folder whose name starts with an underscore, but you should verify this is the case with your installation of IIS. If you're running Apache, or another web server such as WebSphere, consult the documentation on how to deny permission to such folders. You may also want to contact your IT department.

It goes without saying that securing your web site is important. You should not rely on the encryption in the `contribute.xml` *file alone. You must prevent visitors from browsing folders that start with an underscore. Do not simply change the permissions of the* _mm *folder. There are other folders that should also be secured, such as* _baks *folders and* _notes *folders.* _baks *folders are found within each folder in a site and contain backup copies of pages. The* _notes *folder contains Check In/Check Out notes. These notes list who checked a file out, when they checked it out, and when they checked it in. Changing the security properties through your web server administrator tools is the easiest and most comprehensive way to secure your site. Consult your web server documentation to learn how you can limit browsing of folders.*

If you cannot limit browsing of folders that start with an underscore, consider creating a development environment for your web site. A development environment is a separate site that your contributors modify. In such a model, contributors do not edit files on the live server, but rather a separate, testing server. Approved files are then moved to the live server at some later time, and without the Contribute folders.

If you're a Dreamweaver MX user, you should be aware that Dreamweaver MX creates a folder called _mmServerScripts that contains files associated with the application platform you're running (for example, ColdFusion, ASP, and so on). These files may contain sensitive information about your server, and should never be published to a live environment.

Web Site Folder Structure

The design of your site's folder structure will influence how you manage your Contribute users. If you already have a live site, then some of the following information won't be of much use, the assumption being that you're not going to redesign your site's structure to accommodate Contribute users. That said, you should still read this section because it will help you understand how Contribute approaches site administration. If you're starting a site from scratch, carefully consider how your site's folder design will affect the administration of Contribute users. While you should not design your site structure around Contribute, managing users should be taken into consideration.

There are numerous ways to design a site's folder structure. How you design the structure depends on a number of factors, but the following are typical considerations:

- **Organization structure**: Many sites are designed around the structure of an organization. The typical Org Chart design is not a good choice for most sites, although corporate intranets may benefits from such a design

- **Site function**: Designing a site's structure by considering what a visitor does on your site is difficult, but if done correctly, can make your site easier to use. Many corporate web sites use such an organization. For example, such a site might be organized by general heading such as: Products, Support, Contact, and so on. Within each of these folders, there may exist additional folders

- **Site contributors**: Many sites have numerous content contributors. You may consider organizing your site around the various groups that control content on the site. Like basing a design on your organization's reporting structure, this works well for intranets

Site Size

Small sites typically use a flat structure. While such sites may use folders to organize content, typically there are few if any nested folders. Large sites, on the other hand, may use numerous nested folders. The size of your site and its structure will help determine how you manage permission groups in Contribute. In general, a flat or shallow site structure will limit the control you have over Contribute users, because Contribute permissions are set at the folder level, not the file level. The fewer folders you have in your site, the fewer options you have when creating permission groups. In the following sections, we will discuss strategies for setting up and managing user groups according to the structure of your site.

Flat and Shallow Sites

Small sites with flat structures, especially those with few or no folders, are difficult to manage using Contribute. Contribute enables you to associate users with folders, but you cannot restrict access to files through Contribute. Therefore, if your site structure is flat, like the following figure, you will not be able to associate permission groups with folders of your site. In the following example, users will have access to all files within the root folder of the site. The best you can do is create one group and associate that group with the root level of the web site.

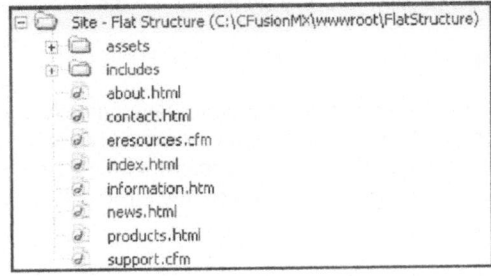

A flat file structure site

If your current site looks similar to the structure shown above, you should consider reorganizing it. Not only will you be able to create permission groups in Contribute and associate those groups with folders, but reorganizing your site will help you manage site files as well. If you do decide to reorganize your site, be sure to test it before launch. Moving files around, even within Dreamweaver, may introduce problems such as broken links.

A flat site structure like the one above is uncommon. Most small sites use at least a single level of folders to organize content. With a shallow site structure, one with a single layer of folders, you can associate users with individual folders. If we reorganize the site above by creating folders that hold different types of content, as seen in the next figure, it becomes much easier to locate content as your site grows.

Perhaps more importantly, restructuring the site enables you to create permission groups and associate these groups with individual folders within the site. For example, we can create a group that consists of the employees within the public relations department, and give them permission to modify files within the PR folder. In this scenario, employees within the public relations department could not create, edit, or delete content within any folder other than PR, nor could they modify content at the root level of the site.

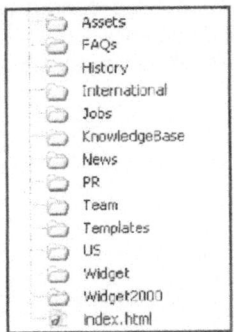

A site with multiple folders

We're not restricted to associating a permission group with a single folder. If the public relations department were responsible for writing news stories, we could add the News folder to their permissions. The public relations department could then edit files within the News and PR folders. In addition, we can associate multiple permission groups to a single folder. If the marketing group also created news stories, we could create a permission group called Marketing and give the group permission to edit pages within the News folder. Both the public relations group and the marketing group could modify files within the News folder, but only the public relations group could modify files within the PR folder because we did not give the Marketing group permissions on the PR folder. As you can see, permission groups can be flexible, but only as flexible as the design of the site folder structure.

Distributed Sites

Large public web sites or intranets may be set up to have multiple administrators. Sites such as these are made up of multiple small sites, each with its own administrator(s). If Dreamweaver is used on such a site, each mini-site within the main site may contain its own templates folder, assets folder, and so on, as seen next. If your site conforms to this structure, you will need to create multiple site definitions.

You cannot nest Contribute sites within one another. In other words, given the example below, you cannot define the root as a site and define each smaller site within the root as a separate site. The solution is to define each mini-site as its own separate Contribute site. Each site will require an administrator. You can define yourself as the administrator for each site and create permission groups for each site. In addition, you can add administrators to each mini-site. For example, you can add someone from the public relations group as an administrator for the *About Us* mini-site. Both you and the member of the public relations department could then manage permission groups, change site-wide settings, and so on.

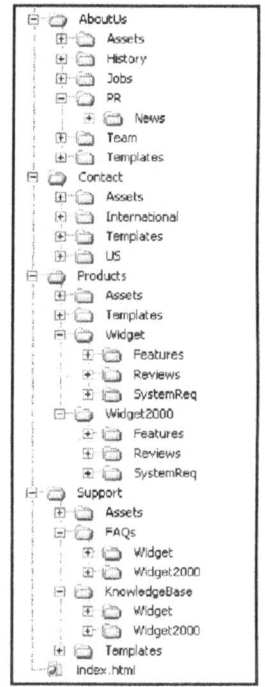

This flexibility is useful when working with large sites that have contributors spread across a large organization. As the person charged with managing your site, you could pass the responsibility of managing permission groups to the departments themselves, freeing you to work on other projects such as application development. Of course, this solution only works if those managing their individual sites are competent. There is no right or wrong solution – it's up to you.

In the example on the right there are many "mini-sites" within the root site. Each site, such as support, products, and so on, contains its own set of templates. If this example is similar to your own site, you must define each "mini-site" as a separate site because you cannot nest Contribute site definitions. Therefore, this site would be defined as four separate mini-sites in Contribute: the *AboutUs*, *Contact*, *Products*, and *Support* sites.

A site containing multiple mini-sites

Creating an Administrator Account...

The first step in managing a site with Contribute is to create an administrator account. When you create the administrator account, Contribute will automatically set up your site, placing the necessary folders and files on the server.

In order to integrate Dreamweaver MX and Contribute, you will need to update Dreamweaver MX to the patched release, as this includes all the Contribute-related additions. It can be downloaded at: http://www.macromedia.com/softw are/dreamweaver/special/updater/.

...Through Dreamweaver

The update adds an additional category, Contribute, under the *Advanced* tab in the *Site Definition* dialog box.

In order to enable Contribute-compatibility to a defined site in Dreamweaver MX, you must verify that the site conforms to these requirements:

The site has Remote Info defined as something other than None: If Contribute is to be used with a site, the *Remote Info* is typically set to either FTP or Local/Network, although you can use another *Remote Info* definition in Dreamweaver, for example, RDS. If you're using FTP or Local/Network, the connection settings defined within Dreamweaver MX can be shared with Contribute users. In other words, the FTP host, login, and password can be shared with your users and will be used when creating connection keys. Contribute users will not have direct access to the information stored in the connection key. Information such as FTP host, login, and password are encrypted in the connection key. This helps protect that sensitive information.

The following section assumes that you have a site defined in Dreamweaver. If you do not, refer to the Dreamweaver MX documentation on defining a site. Since most web professionals prefer the Advanced Site Definition option, the following directions assume that the Advanced tab is selected in the Site Definition window. If you use the Basic tab, a wizard walks you through the creation of your site, but you will need to click on the Advanced tab and select the Contribute category to enable Contribute for a site.

If you use a *Remote Info* definition other than FTP or Local/Network, you will need to customize the connection setting before creating connection keys. In other words, you will need to define how Contribute users connect to the web site, since they cannot use the connection method you use in Dreamweaver MX.

Check In and Check Out must be enabled: Contribute uses Dreamweaver's mechanism to lock files while they're being edited. So it must be enabled in Dreamweaver in order for the site to be compatible with Contribute. In the *Remote Info* category, check *Enable File Check In and Check Out*. You must specify a *Check Out Name* and *E-mail Address*. The check out name and e-mail address are displayed in Contribute (and Dreamweaver MX) when a file is checked out by another user. *Check In* and *Check Out* are features of Dreamweaver: other applications, such as Adobe GoLive or Microsoft FrontPage do not recognize Dreamweaver's file-locking system.

The *Remote Info* dialog box should look similar to the following screenshot:

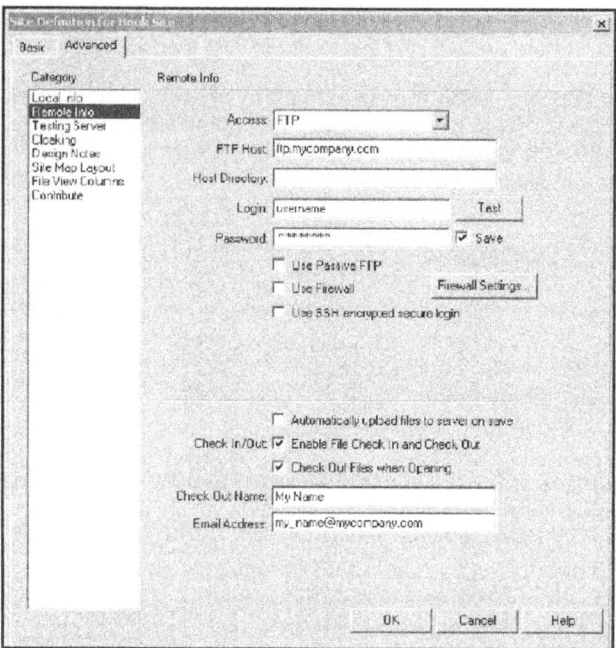

An example of remote information for a Contribute-enabled site

Design notes must also be enabled. In addition, the *Upload Design Note For Sharing* option must be checked. A Contribute-enabled site uses design notes to keep track of who checks out a file for editing and when they checked it out. This information enables you to trace the history of a file. It is also used with the rollback feature. To enable design notes, select the *Design Notes* category in the *Site Definition* dialog box and check both boxes in the right pane, as seen to the right:

The Design Notes window

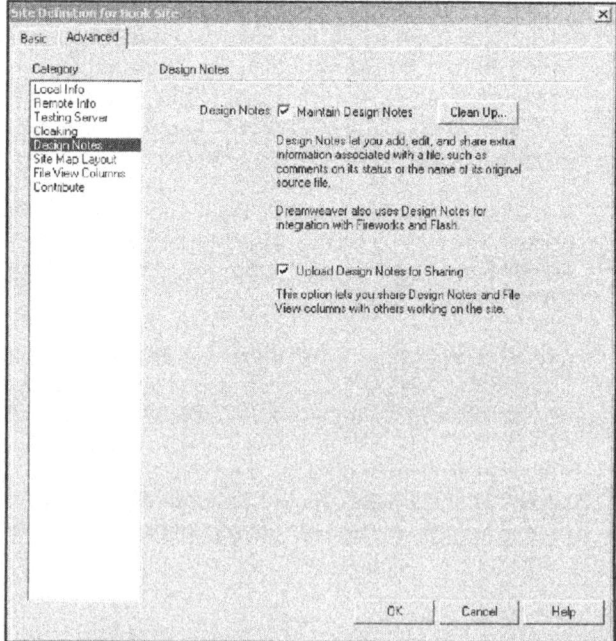

Once the options listed above are enabled, check the *Enable Contribute Compatibility* in the *Contribute* Category. Your site is now Contribute-enabled and two new options are listed in the *Contribute* category, *Site Root URL* and *Administration*. The *Site Root URL* textbox should be completed already. If it isn't, click on the *Local Info* category and verify that the *HTTP Address* textbox is completed correctly. If it isn't, enter the HTTP address of your web site. This is the root address of the site.

Click the *Administer Website* button in the Contribute category. You are told that the site does not have a Contribute Administrator, and Dreamweaver MX asks if you want to administrate the site. Click *Yes*.

The password dialog

You must choose an administrator password for the site. This is not the FTP or network password. This is the password administrators must supply in order to change the Contribute settings. You will be prompted for this password each time you administer the site, so don't lose it.

...Through Contribute

To create an administrator account for a web site from Contribute, choose *Edit > My Connections*, and click the *New* button in the *My Connections* dialog box. The *Connection Wizard* opens and walks you through the process of creating a new site connection.

The first page of the wizard asks if you have a connection key; you can safely ignore this and click *Next*.

The next page of the wizard asks you for your name and e-mail address. This information is used for *Check In/Check Out*. Since *Check In/Check Out* and *Design Notes* are required in order to use Contribute, you do not have to enable them manually as you did in Dreamweaver.

The second page of the wizard requires you to enter the URL for your web site. This is the web address for the site, which in the case of a distributed site is not necessarily the root address. Using the earlier example, if you are creating a connection to the *Products* mini-site, you would enter *http://www.mycompany.com/products/*, and not the root address of *http://www.mycompany.com/*.

In the third page of the wizard you provide connection information. If you're connecting via FTP, you must supply the FTP name for the server along with the login name and password. The FTP name should not include folder information. If we use the large site example, as we did above, the FTP name is *ftp.mycompany.com*, and not *ftp.mycompany.com/products/*. Contribute resolves the folder information.

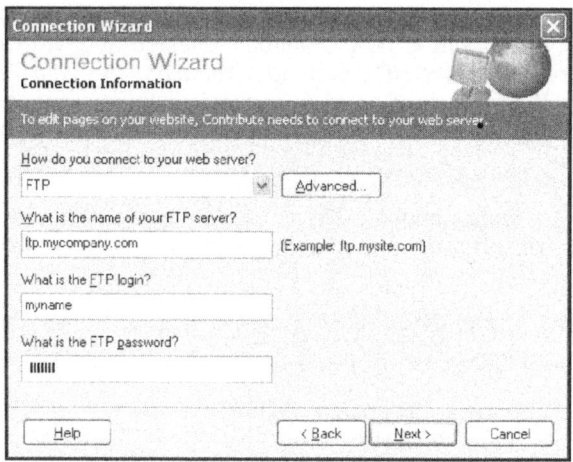

The connection wizard showing FTP information

You need only one FTP account to use Contribute. All users can share the same account because Contribute controls what files users have access to through permission groups. The FTP information you enter will not be available to users.

You may want to create individual accounts via your FTP server software for each Contribute permission group or create separate accounts for each Contribute permission group. The decision is up to you.

If you select *Local/Network* instead of *FTP*, you simply browse to the network location of the files by clicking on the *Choose* button. In this instance, you should browse to the folder where the site files are located, even if you're creating a connection to a large, distributed site. If we use the same example, the location might look like this: \\networkDrive\root\products\.

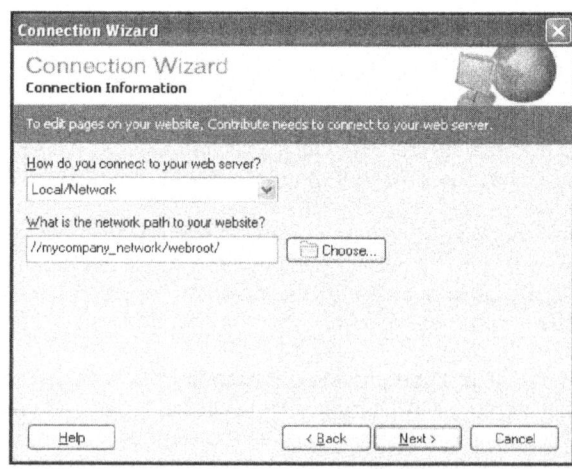

The connection wizard showing local/network folder information

On the final page of the wizard, you choose which permission group you belong to. Since this is the first time a connection is being created to the site, you're asked whether or not you want to be the administrator for the site. Select the *Yes, I Want To Be The Administrator*. Two textboxes are displayed.

You must choose an administrator password for the site. As noted above, this is not the FTP or network password. This is the password administrators must supply in order to change the site settings.

At the end of the wizard a summary of the connection information is displayed. Verify that the information is correct and click *Done*. Close the *My Connections* window. Whether you create a connection using Dreamweaver MX or Contribute, the end result is the same. You are now the administrator for the site. As the administrator, your first job is to create permission groups.

Unlike Dreamweaver MX, Contribute doesn't allow you to name your site when you run the Connection Wizard. By default, Contribute names the site using the title of the site's homepage. It's a good idea to rename the site once it's created, especially if the site's homepage title is descriptive.

Administering a Site

When you create a new connection in Contribute or Dreamweaver MX, you are asked whether you want to administer the site. Answering yes to the question, and entering the site's administrator password, opens the *Administer Website* window. You can also access the *Administer Website* window by choosing *Edit > Administer Website > name of the site* in Contribute.

From the *Administer Website* window, you can change *Sitewide* settings, manage permission groups, and set up users. *Sitewide* settings are options that apply to the entire site, such as enabling rollbacks, and changing the administrator e-mail and password. Managing permission groups includes creating groups, setting group permissions, and controlling the behavior Contribute exhibits when users edit pages. Setting up users includes creating connection keys and distributing them to users.

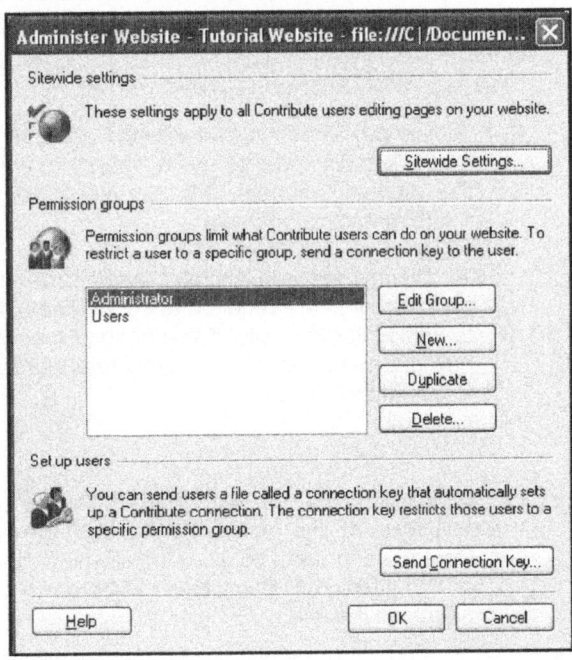

The Administer Site window

Sitewide Settings

Sitewide settings control the way Contribute behaves for all users, including the administrator. Changing any setting in the *Sitewide Settings* window changes the setting for everyone connecting to the site through Contribute.

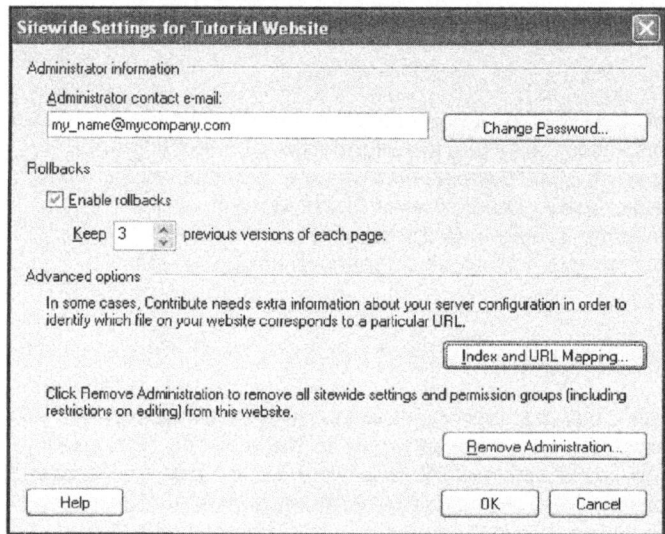

The Sitewide Settings window

Administrator Information

To change the Administrator e-mail address, simply type a new address into the textbox. This e-mail address is displayed to users when they encounter problems using Contribute, so make sure that the address is correct. Once an e-mail address is changed, all Contribute users will see the new address within Contribute.

To change the administrator password, click on the *Change Password* button. To change the password you are required to supply the old password. The old password is the password you use to administer your site. If you change the password, you must notify all other administrators of the new password, because administrators are prompted for the site password each time they attempt to administer the site.

Rollbacks

Rollbacks are a *Site-wide* feature. You cannot enable or disable rollbacks at the permission group level so if it's enabled, Contribute creates backups of all pages that are edited on the site. In addition, Dreamweaver MX creates backups when editing pages on the site.

Page rollbacks are only available after a Contribute user publishes a page. If the user saves a page for later, the rollback will not be available.

To enable rollbacks, check *Enable Rollbacks* and set the number of rollbacks by entering a number into the textbox below. You can store up to 99 versions of a single published page. Carefully consider how many rollbacks you will need, and how many versions of each page your web server can store. If your site is large, and is updated frequently, even the smallest pages can eat disk space when a large number of rollbacks are allowed.

Index and URL Mapping

When Contribute connects to a web server directory it searches the folder for an index page. The **Index Files** list in the *Index and URL Mapping* window enables you to specify what kind of index pages Contribute should look for, and the order in which it should look. You can add, edit, and remove index files from the list by selecting the file and clicking on the appropriate button. You move index files up and down within the list by selecting the file and clicking on the up or down button.

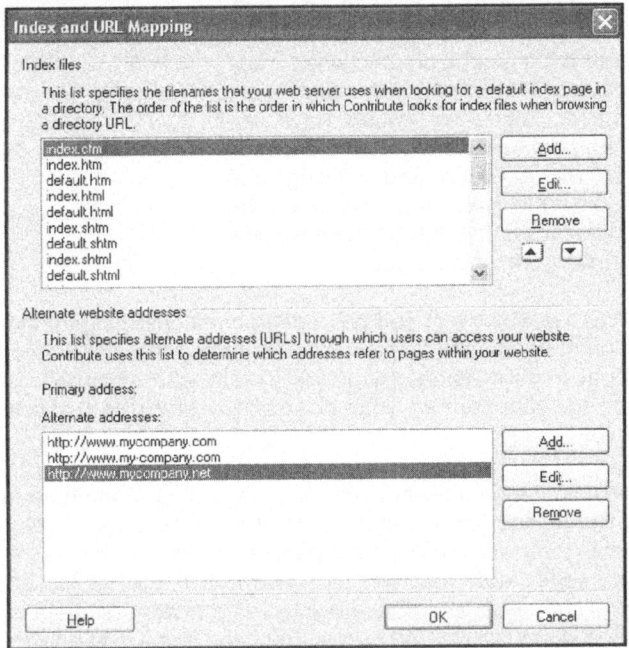

The Index and URL Mapping window

For example, if your site is entirely ColdFusion-based, and you use `index.cfm` as the index page for directories, you should move `index.cfm` to the top of the *Index Files* list. Doing so will force Contribute to look for `index.cfm` first when connecting to a web directory. If no `index.cfm` is present then Contribute will look for the next file type on the list.

If your site uses multiple addresses, such as *www.mycompany.com*, *www.my-company.com*, and *www.mycompany.net*, and they all point to the same web site, you should add the additional web site addresses to the *Alternate Website Addresses* list in the *Index and URL Mapping* window. Not adding the alternative addresses may cause unpredictable results when users edit pages with Contribute, especially if they attempt to connect to the site through an alternate address.

Remove Administration

The last option listed under *Advanced Options* is *Remove Administration*. Choosing this option removes all permission groups, including the administrator group, from the site. Since all permission groups are removed, any restrictions placed on users are also removed. Removing administration deletes the `Contribute.xml` file from the _mm folder. It does not delete the _mm folder, and all notes and rollback versions (`.BAK` files) are kept.

Permission Groups

As described earlier, **permission groups** define the level of access Contribute users have to assets on your web site. To create a permission group, open the *Administer Website* window. You can add, edit, duplicate, or delete permission groups. By default, there are two permission groups created when a site is Contribute-enabled: the *Administrator* and *Users* permission groups. All sites must have an administrator group, but the users group is optional. Selecting a permission group and clicking *Edit Group*, or clicking on the *New* button will open the *Permission Group* window. It is through this window that you administrate permission groups.

This chapter does not explain all of the options found in the Permission Group window because some are explained in greater detail in later chapters of the book. Please refer to Chapter 5 for more information and tips on setting permission group options (we've included specific information on setting up your site so that it conforms to accessibility standards and W3C recommendations.)

The *Permission Group* window contains six categories of setting that you can modify. Unlike site-wide settings, changing options within these six categories only affects a particular permission group. The number of permission groups you create, and what permissions you give them can, relate directly to the structure of your site, as we discussed above in the *Web Site Folder Structure* section.

Perhaps the most common misunderstanding regarding Contribute relates to how users are managed. Contribute **does not** manage users; it manages groups. You do not add users to your permission groups. Permission groups are general categories of users that are used to define how groups of users interact with your site. For example, if your Sales department consists of four employees, Cindy, John, Bob, and Sue and you create a permission group for Sales, you do not add the four employees to the group. Cindy, John, Bob, and Sue are in no way associated with the Sales permission group within Contribute. Therefore, Cindy, John, Bob, and Sue connect to the site through Contribute as Sales group, not as individuals.

General Permissions

The **General** permission settings are used to describe the permission group. The description is displayed to users if they try to join a group. If you have a large site, with many permission groups, it's a good idea to write detailed descriptions of the group. Detailed descriptions help users and administrators keep track of the types of permission groups associated with a site.

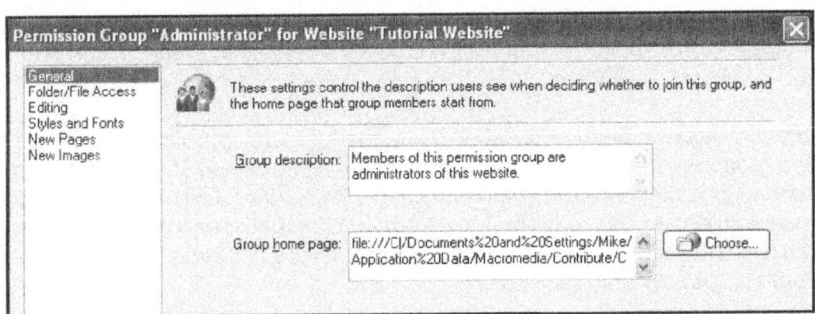

The General Permissions tab

Make sure you give a detailed description of the permission group you're creating because it makes your job easier when you're managing a large site, and helps users who are joining the group.

Folder/File Access Permissions

The *Folder/File Access* category is perhaps the most important category when it comes to setting permissions. It is in this window that you restrict a permission group's access to folders. By default, a permission group can edit any file on the site; therefore, if you want to restrict a permission group's access to files, you must check *Only Allow Editing Within These Folders*. You can then add the folders which the group can edit by clicking the *Add Folder* button. For example, if you create a permission group called *Marketing* and want to restrict their editing permissions to only the News, Team, and History folders, you would do it in the *Folder/File Access* category.

Folder permissions cascade down to subfolders. For example, if you give the Sales group permission to edit files within the Products folder, and the Products folder contains two subfolders: WidgetXP and Widget2000, the Sales groups can edit any file located within the Products/WidgetXP and Products/Widget2000 folders.

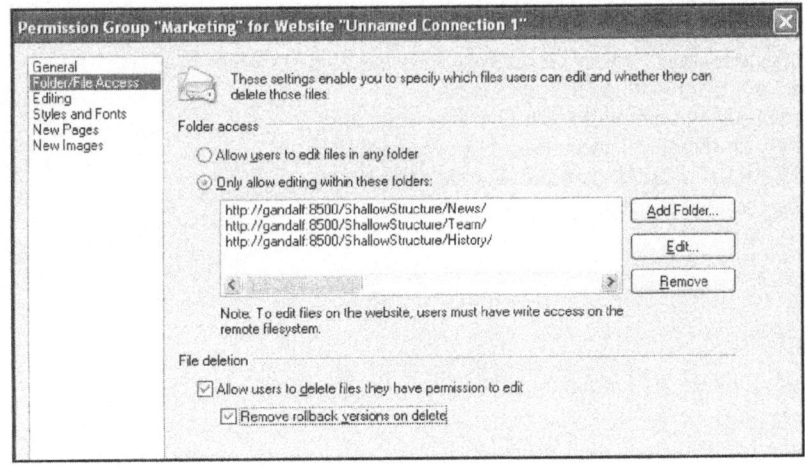

The Folder/File Access tab

You restrict a permission group's access to folders through the *Folder/File Access* category. In addition, you allow or deny them permission to delete files from the folder you have given them access to.

The *Folder/File Access* category is where you grant groups permission to delete files. By default, permission groups are not allowed to delete files from the server. If you want permission groups to be able to delete files, check the *Allow Users To Delete Files They Have Permission To Edit* – this enables users to delete files only from folders they have permission to access. As with any system that allows users to delete files, it's a good idea to have a separate backup system running, just in case something catastrophic happens.

By default, rollback versions of files are not deleted when a file is deleted. Therefore, users can restore a deleted file if a rollback version exists. Checking *Remove Rollback Version On Delete* will delete the rollback files located in the _baks folder when a file is deleted. If you're concerned about storage space on your site, checking this is a good idea. Just remember that, if it is checked and a user deletes a file, there are no backups that you can restore.

Editing Permissions

If you're concerned about enforcing HTML standards-compliance on your site, the *Editing* category is an important window. From this window, you dictate how Contribute will behave when a user from a permission group uses the program. In addition, you can take it a step further and only allow users to edit text on a page.

If you check *Only Allow Text Editing And Formatting*, users can only edit text; they cannot add or modify links, images, or tables, although they can modify text within a table. This is a useful option if users will only be making small text changes. If users need to create entire pages, you should enable *Allow Unrestricted Editing*, which is the default setting. If *Allow Unrestricted Editing* is checked, it is strongly recommended that *Protect Scripts And Forms* also be checked. By checking *Protect Scripts And Forms*, you ensure that Contribute will not overwrite form, scripting, or dynamic code found on the page. If unchecked, Contribute users can accidentally delete scripting by deleting objects found on the page.

Contribute is based on the Dreamweaver MX engine, and because of this, the code that it produces should conform to the HTML document type defined on the page. That said, if you enable/disable certain features in Contribute, your code may not be valid. You must balance the ease-of-use features found in Contribute against the needs of your organization. If standards-compliant, structurally sound code is important, you may need to offer additional training to your Contribute users.

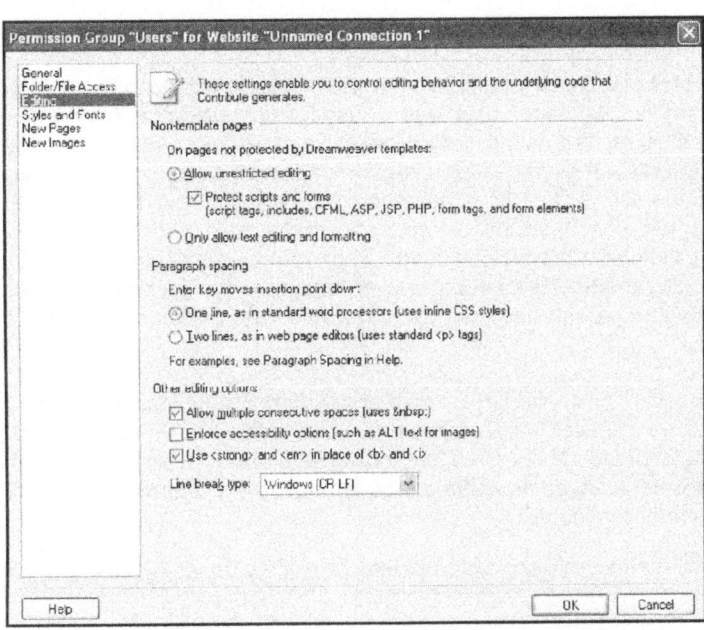

The editing category enables you to control the code that Contribute writes.

Paragraph Spacing and *Other Editing Options* are designed to make Contribute more user-friendly to non-technical users. You should refer to *Chapter 5*, for more information on how to use these options.

Styles and Fonts Permissions

Contribute allows you to permit users to format text through stylesheets, the `<font>` tag, or both. In the *Styles And Fonts* category you choose how a permission group can format text. If standards-compliance is important, you'll want to disable the use of the `<font>` tag. If ease-of-use is more important than standards-compliance, you should allow users to apply formatting using the `<font>` tag. Enabling the use of the `<font>` tag makes Contribute act more like a word processor, which most of your users will be familiar with. By default, the `<font>` tag is enabled. Like all options within Contribute, you can enable or disable the use of the `<font>` tag at any time. If you change a setting, users see the change the next time they open a file from the site in Contribute. Contribute will not update formatting from one kind to another, so it is important that you are consistent from the start.

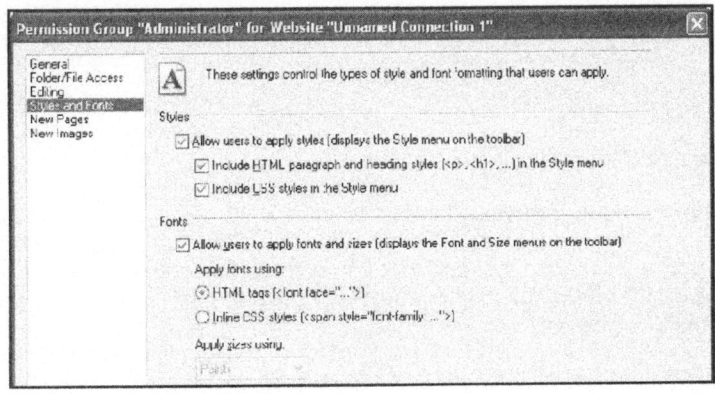

The Styles and Fonts tab

New Pages Permissions

Contribute users can create pages in a number of ways. They can create a blank page, use sample pages, copy an existing page on the site, or use Dreamweaver templates. If consistency is important to your organization, then you should disable the ability to create blank pages. You should also not allow users to create new pages from sample pages. Allowing users to create new pages based on the current page allows Contribute users to create a page based on pages they have permission to edit. For example, the Sales department can only create pages based on pages that are stored within folders they have permission to edit. Therefore, users cannot browse the Web and create new pages based on random sites. Dreamweaver templates are the best way to ensure a consistent look and feel throughout a site because you can lock down portions of the page so that users cannot modify them.

Contribute is compatible with Dreamweaver MX and Dreamweaver 4 templates. All of the features available in Dreamweaver MX templates, such as locking down regions and repeating regions, are available to Contribute. Of course, Contribute users cannot edit templates. It is the responsibility of the Web professional to create and manage templates in Dreamweaver. For more information on this topic, please refer to *Chapter 7*.

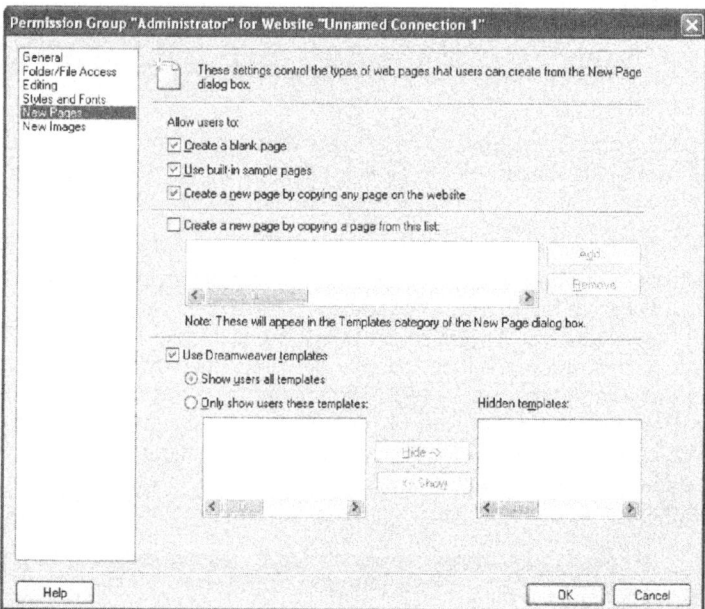

The New Pages tab

New Images Permissions

The last category in the *Permission Group* window is the *New Images* category. The only option in this category is to limit the file size of new images users add to a page. Since most of your users will not be tech-savvy, it is recommended that you enforce some size limitation. It is not uncommon for users to insert a 200KB image into a page. Setting a size limit will not allow them to insert an image larger than the size you set.

Users may not understand why they cannot insert large images, so explaining to them why they should not insert large files is important. You may also want to consider training them on how to reduce image file size.

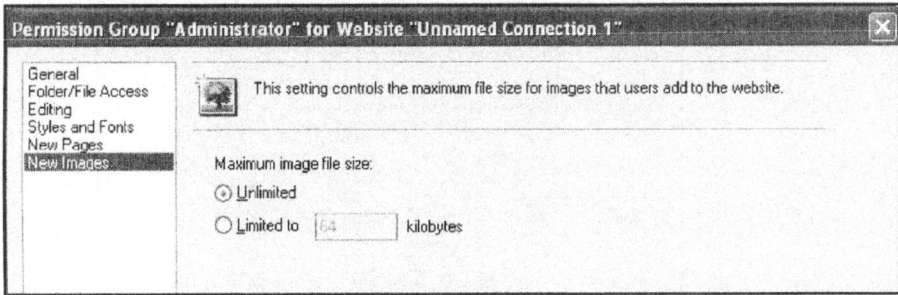

The New Images tab

Setting up Users

Up until now we've discussed how to administer a Contribute site by creating accounts and permission groups. At this stage, your users are still unable to create and update content. You must now set up your user's copies of Contribute so that they can edit web site content. You can visit each Contribute users and set them up one at a time, but that would take a long time if you're part of a large organization. Fortunately, Contribute allows you to create connection keys.

Connection keys make the process of setting up multiple users much easier. Connection keys are created for individual permission groups. You create a key and e-mail it directly to members of a permission group. The connection key is encrypted and requires users to know the password (created when you create the key), to open it. Once a user opens the key in Contribute and supplies the correct password, Contribute reads the information contained in the key and connects to the site. Once connected, Contribute follows the permission group settings defined by the administrator.

To create a connection key click on the *Send Connection Key* button in the *Administer Website* window (in either Dreamweaver MX or Contribute). A wizard starts that walks you through the process of creating a key.

Choose whether you want to send the current connection setting or customize the connection settings. If you choose to send the current settings and you're using an FTP connection, you can include the FTP settings in the connection key. Since the connection key is encrypted, users receiving the key will not be able to read the FTP login and password. If you choose to customize the connection, you are prompted to enter customized connection information for the key. This is useful if you want a permission group to connect to the web site using an FTP login other than the login used by the administrator, as seen next:

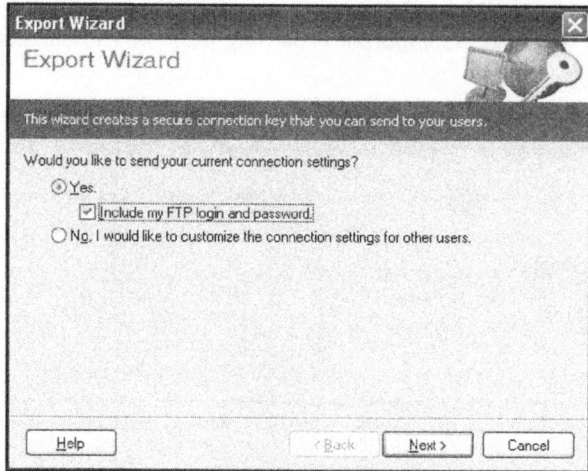

The export wizard

Select the permission group you are creating a key for. A description of the group is displayed in the right pane.

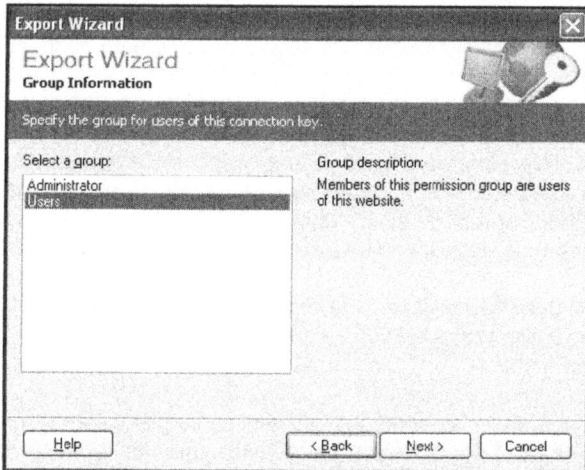

The export wizard showing the permission groups

Set the password for the key and e-mail the key or save it to your local machine. If you choose to e-mail the key, your e-mail application will open with the connection key file attached to the new e-mail. Additionally, Contribute places generic instructions on opening the connection key file within the message of the e-mail. The password you create is used for the connection key only.

The connection key contains only connection information. None of the permission group settings are sent in the key. Permission group settings are stored on the server. Contribute reads the permission group settings when it connects to the server. Therefore, if the site administrator changes a group's permissions, Contribute will observe the changes. You do not need to resend a connection key when you change permissions.

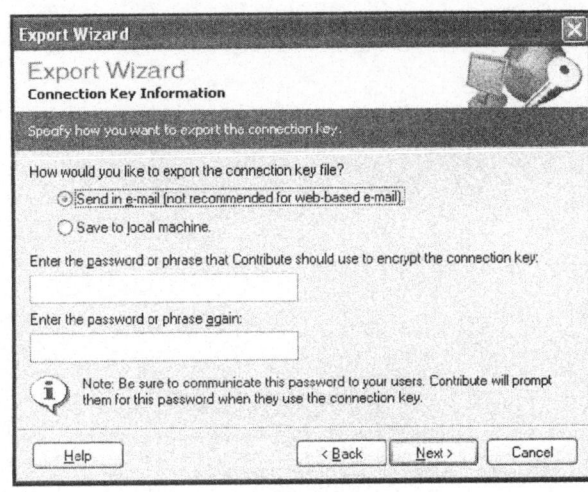

Creating a password for the connection key

If you create multiple permission groups and support many Contribute authors, mailing individual connection keys can be a chore. It is recommended that you save connection keys to your local machine or to a network location. Doing so enables you to resend the key as you add users to a permission group without having to regenerate it.

Individual users are not associated with permission groups. Permission groups are a generalized group with certain permissions defined by the administrator. If a member of your organization leaves the company, you cannot simply remove that person from a permission group. If a user leaves your organization, and you want to make sure they cannot connect to your site through Contribute from another location, you must delete the permission group the individual belonged to.

Summary

In this chapter we:

- Discussed how Contribute approaches site management
- Explored various technologies employed by Contribute to set group permissions, set up sites, and manage content
- Learned how to set ourselves up as site administrators, and create Permission Groups
- Set editing and file permissions and created connection keys for our Permission Groups

We covered a lot of options within a short chapter but all of the options that were glossed over will be explored in more detail in later chapters.

3

In this Chapter

- Working with images and hyperlinks

- Working with non-HTML documents, such as Word and Excel documents

Author: Bill Barrett

Links, Images, and non-HTML Documents

Now that you're up to speed on how to administer a site with Contribute, your content editors are immediately able to begin manipulating content. In a matter of minutes content contributors go from perhaps having zero web skills to having the ability to add text, links, images, and other content to their web sites. There will be a huge rush of excitement for your editors, but I suspect that you will have mixed feelings about the convenience Contribute brings and the havoc which could be wreaked on your site with a new content contribution tool in the hands of non-web-savvy and over-eager editors.

In this chapter we'll focus on how Contribute handles links, images, and other non-HTML documents – in terms of what capabilities Contribute offers the user, as well as how Contribute affects your existing markup and creates its own.

Despite Contribute's very gentle learning curve, there are still some issues that do not become clear without some experimentation, and can cause annoying changes to your code and site structure. This chapter will offer some insight into how Contribute affects the markup in your pages. Some of the questions we'll answer are:

- How can users work with hyperlinks?
- Can users edit client-side image maps?
- Where did the images go when I published a page with new images?
- How do does Contribute handle linking to a PDF, or other file?
- How well does Contribute import Word or Excel documents?
- Can a user import or link to non-HTML objects?

In general, the more functional, dynamic, and cleanly coded your site is, the more you will need to pay particular attention to these issues. Developers administering less formalized or personal web sites will for the most part be able to rely on a judicious choice of Contribute's administrative settings to provide relatively solid markup without the need for much training. It's safe to assume, however, that your editors will ask for more functionality than Contribute is capable of safely delivering, given your development requirements. Knowing the capabilities and practical limits of Contribute will serve you well as you negotiate the balance between your needs and the needs of your content contributors.

Contribute's Document and Images Directories

Before we delve into the intricacies of links, images, and non-HTML files, we need to have an understanding of a couple of Contribute's basic organization principles. Contribute has a system to manage the many possible files that may be uploaded to your web server that eliminates confusion and the possibility of lost or overwritten files. The system creates `/documents` and `/images` directories inside any directory into which a new or edited page is published. For instance, if you published a page with images and a PDF inside `/store/new/`, Contribute would create `/store/new/documents/` and `/store/new/images/` if they don't already exist.

One big reason for handling files this way has to do with user privileges. If individual content contributors are going to manage pages where they upload new images and related documents, and at the same time you have to control access to certain areas of the site, it may not be feasible to store images or documents in a central location. In fact, it is fairly standard among web developers to keep assets close to their pages – that is, to put images and files related to a page in the same directory or in directories under that page, a notable exception being global items used site-wide or in templates.

If you do have a developer whose job it is to specifically create certain kinds of content, for instance Flash movies or PDFs, you can create a central directory for those files such as `/flash` or `/pdfs`. The benefit of this would be to eliminate the unnecessary distribution and "scattering" of similar types of files. Content contributors would always know where to look for Flash or PDF files, and there would then be no duplicate files in different directories should those files be linked to more than one page.

Contribute Naming Conventions

Files that Contribute uploads to the server retain their filename as long as there is no other file in the upload directory with the same name. If Contribute encounters a duplicate name, it will add a series of three numbers, starting with 000. For example, if an image already exists called `kitty.jpg` and another image named `kitty.jpg` is then published, that image will be uploaded as `kitty_000.jpg`, a further `kitty.jpg` will be uploaded as `kitty_001.jpg`, and so forth.

When a file has not been named, Contribute will use the name of the parent file and append the appropriate 3-digit number in the same fashion. This method, while erring on the side of caution in protecting your files, does have the potential to dramatically increase disk use on the server as well as causing confusion with many odd filenames floating around. If you have limited server space for your web site, you will want to monitor the image directories a little more closely than you normally might in order to rid the server of unused images or documents.

Working with Hyperlinks

There are several ways to add links in Contribute, most of which are fairly straightforward for the user. Linking in Contribute, though, is somewhat different from what you are accustomed to, even if you're used to Dreamweaver. we'll review each method below, along with any unique issues or questions arising from that method.

Built-in Linking Methods

The linking methods discussed below are accessed by using the *Link* button in the toolbar, *Insert > Link*, or by choosing *Format > Link Properties*. The *Link Properties* dialog box is shown here:

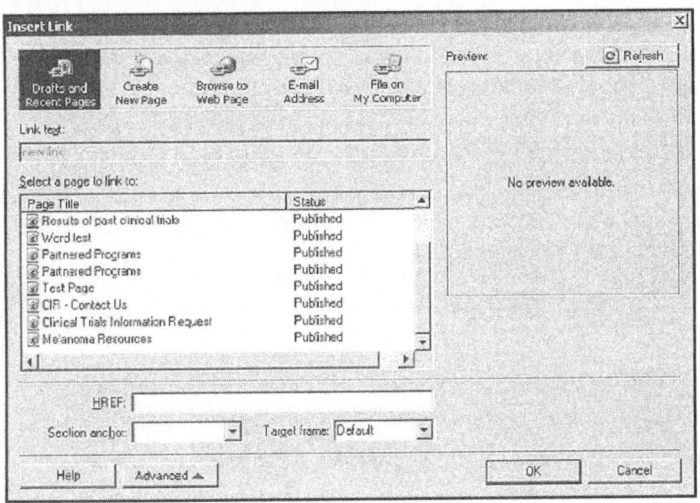

The Insert Link dialog box

Drafts and Recent Pages

This method allows you to choose from a list of draft pages for linking. Contribute will display a complete list of current drafts for you to link to and stores a list of the last ten pages published on your web site. This option makes good sense when working on several related pages on the same site.

This method is good in principle, but its implementation can prove troublesome. There is no way to clear the history of recent pages, and this is annoying if you edit more than one site, because *all* of your sites' previous pages, most likely with no relation to one another, appear in the list together. Also, if the same page is edited more than once in close succession, it will appear in the list twice, creating more clutter and confusion.

Create New Page

A user with the correct permissions can create a new page to link to a current draft page. Contribute saves the current page as a draft and at the same time creates (and switches to) a new draft page. When the new page is published, the original draft page is also published.

As a developer you may fear that stray pages will be published on the server if a draft with a link to a new page is published without the new page being added, thereby creating a broken link. Contribute circumvents this worry by creating a fail-safe: a dialog box informs users that they cannot publish the original page with its newly linked page unless they publish both pages simultaneously.

It's important, especially if you are working directly on the production web server, to have all other edits completed on the original draft before creating the newly linked page. This will avoid accidental publication of the original (unfinished) page while publishing the new page. If the user realizes that they would be publishing an unfinished draft of the original page along with the new page, they can cancel the command to publish and switch to the other draft to complete edits. Doing this, however, invites confusion for the user and can result in orphan pages if the link to the new draft page is modified on the original draft page and then both are published.

Browse to Web Page

This is the easiest and most intuitive way to link to a page. Contribute's *Browse to Link* feature allows you to actually use a mini-browser in the *Link Properties* panel to find (and view) an existing web page (on your site or an external site) for linking:

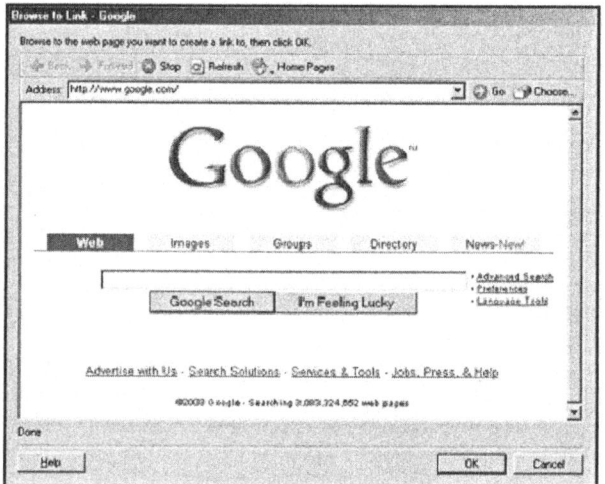

The Browse to Web Page option

This method is a bit cumbersome if you know the URL for the page you want to link to, but it has the added benefit of avoiding broken links caused by typos, and presenting the information in a way that is easy for the end user to understand. Contribute creates absolute links to external pages and relative links to pages that are within your own site.

E-mail Addresses

Simple and straightforward, this linking method only asks for an e-mail address that will be attached to specific text or an image. Be sure to impress upon your users that Contribute does not validate (check the form of) or verify (check for the existence of) an e-mail address.

It's also a good idea to warn your editors that e-mail addresses on a web site using the `mailto:` link option are wide open to e-mail harvesters. An alternative solution is to use a web form on a contact page where the e-mail addresses are processed by a server-side script and are not contained in the HTML page itself.

File on My Computer

This is another simple linking method that provides a directory window to browse files on your local hard drive or other drives on your network. Simply choose the file you want to link to and the link will be created.

Some of your contributors may confuse *linking* to a document (for example, a Word file) with *importing or converting* the contents of a document. Linking to a file on the local drive or network creates only a simple HTML hyperlink and does not touch the contents of the document. Contribute will simply upload to the web server the linked document along with the published page. See *Working with other documents* for more information about importing and converting Word or Excel documents into a web page.

If you link to an HTML document that in turn has links to other images, HTML pages, or non-HTML documents on your local drives, Contribute will upload all those files along with the published web page. These files will be placed on the server in either a `/documents` or `/images` directory (as appropriate) inside the directory where the page is being published. Obviously this can cause problems, which we'll discuss in more detail below.

Drag-and-Drop Linking

Almost anything can be linked in Contribute by a simple drag-and-drop operation, whether it is a Flash movie, PDF, image, HTML page, or a non-HTML document. If it is a file format Contribute does not understand, it takes the name of the file and uses that as the link text, which you can change later. Contribute will upload the linked file and its dependencies upon publishing the web page

Linking Issues in Contribute

While the linking facilities found in Contribute are useful, there are a number of issues you should be aware of.

Linking to Files with Many Dependencies

When publishing pages where you have linked to documents on your local drives, Contribute uploads the pages themselves *along with* all other dependent (linked) documents and images. For example, if you link to another HTML page that happens to contain 25 links to different PDFs, Contribute will, along with the HTML page, upload all 25 PDFs as well. This happens only for HTML files; if you link instead to PDF files or Word documents, any dependent hyperlinks within those files are ignored.

The reason for uploading the extra files is, of course, that Contribute is protecting your site from broken links. Content contributors may be confused as to why Contribute seems to be transferring what they may think are random files to the web server. This is especially true of users who are working through a slow dial-up connection, as this facility could lock up their Internet access if there are particularly large dependent files to be uploaded.

If you wish to work in Contribute with a file that has many dependencies but do not want Contribute to automatically upload the dependent files to the server, you must resort to other transfer methods (like FTP) before editing that page in Contribute.

> **.htm versus .html**
>
> Contribute defaults to the `.htm` file extension when creating blank pages. If you prefer `.html` or another extension for your pages, be sure your content contributors are aware that they must specifically modify the file extension before publishing new pages.

How Contribute Writes Links

There are three linking styles in common use: absolute, relative, and root-relative linking. Contribute defaults to relative linking unless it must use an absolute link to connect to an external domain. Many developers use root-relative linking – writing URLs in relation to the root directory of the web server – because it is both convenient to write and allows code to be used anywhere on the web site without further editing. Unfortunately, Contribute does not allow you to specify the type of linking you prefer. In most situations, this should not present a problem, since reusable code will tend to be in your templates and locked regions.

Handling Moved or Deleted Pages

Contribute does not allow a user to move pages to new locations, but it does allow a user to publish a draft of an existing page as a new page – a possible workaround for moving pages. When using the *Publish as New Page...* command, Contribute will modify links as necessary on the new page to avoid broken links. Since Contribute does not have advanced site management features like Dreamweaver MX such as the ability to modify links on other pages when a page is moved independently of Contribute you should be cautious when moving pages manually on the web server; Contribute will not be able to fix broken links caused by ill-conceived page rearranging. Contribute also does not remove links to pages that are deleted; you will end up with a dead link on those pages. You and your users should be sure to perform quality assurance testing regularly on your site, especially after pages are moved or deletions are made.

Client-side Image Maps

Contribute doesn't allow users to add client-side image maps, but does allow the user some manipulation of image map parameters, and surprisingly they are the most dangerous parameters to allow non-technical users to edit. When a page with an image map is opened for editing in Contribute, the locations of the hotspots are visible as blue shaded regions, as shown next:

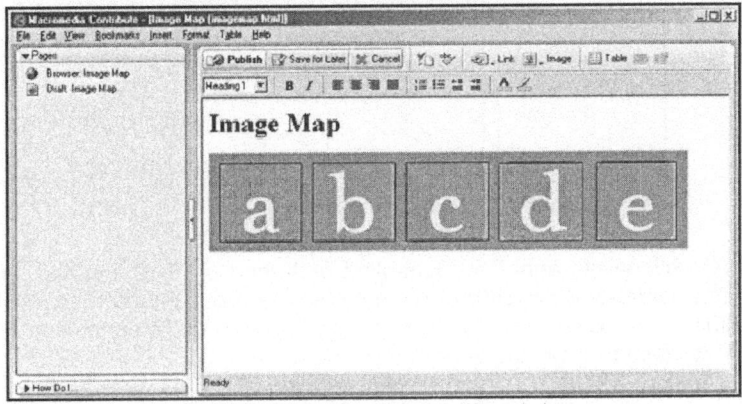

An image map in Contribute's editing window

Below is a summary of what Contribute users can do with image maps. Users can:

- Alter the location of the hotspots or change their shape. Clicking on any part of the shaded region and dragging will move the hotspot to any other part of the image. Dragging the handles will change the shape

- Delete a hotspot entirely by selecting it and pressing *DELETE*

- Delete the entire image map altogether by deleting all the hotspots on the image. When this is done, Contribute deletes all associated markup related to the image map

- Change the actual image with which an image map is associated (and then reposition or resize any existing hotspots)

Here's what users cannot do with image maps:

- Modify the URLs of hotspots

- Add new hotspots to the image map

When a shaded region is clicked, that hotspot is selected and a solid border appears with three or more handles. In the following image, hotspot "b" has been selected, while hotspot "d" has been deleted altogether.

Links, Images, and non-HTML Documents

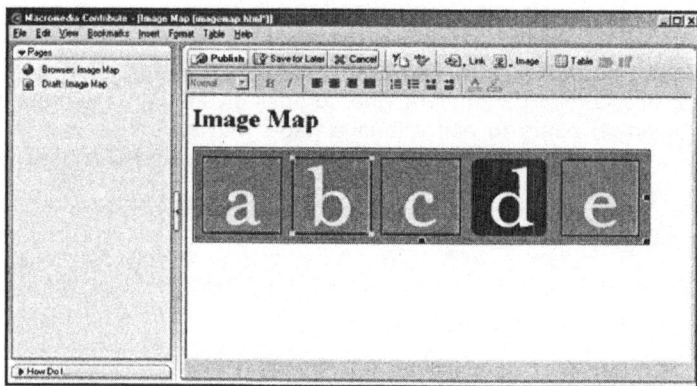

The image map after editing

Image map functionality cannot be controlled or turned off in Contribute 1.0. The only ways a developer can completely protect image maps are to place image maps in locked regions of a template, limit users to text-only editing, or use server-side image maps (which are generally undesirable because they tax the server's performance).

Link Colors

A discussion about linking would not be complete without talking about link colors. Before CSS became the standard for specifying formatting and style decisions, developers used the tags and attributes that had been forced into the HTML specs; specifically, several attributes added to the `<body>` tag to specify page-wide link colors. Now that those attributes are deprecated (though unfortunately still widely in use), link colors should preferably be specified in stylesheets.

If you are administering a site with tightly controlled design specifications, you will probably want to use an external stylesheet that includes the following rules for setting link colors (modify the colors as necessary for your needs):

```
a:link { color: #000099; }
a:visited { color: purple; }
a:active { color: #cc0000; }
```

and optionally (this works in IE4, Netscape 6, and Opera 4 and higher):

```
a:hover { color: orange; }
```

Because of really obscure "specificity" calculations that the CSS parser follows, you need to put these rules in the following order for them to function together properly: `a:link`, `a:visited`, `a:hover`, `a:active`.

If you don't add these rules to your stylesheet, or if you don't use stylesheets at all, be aware that Contribute has provided a way for content editors to specify link colors themselves using the *Page Properties panel (Format > Page Properties or CTRL + J):*

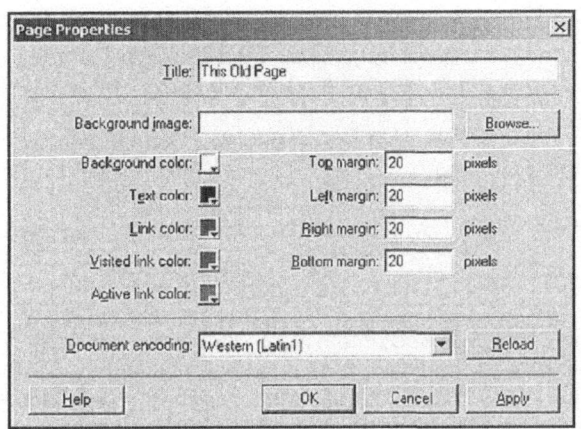

Changing link colors in the Page Properties dialog

The colors section of the *Page Properties* panel adds those deprecated attributes to the `<body>` tag of the page, giving the editors more control of design specifications that you may be willing to cede to them. This happens even if your page's DOCTYPE is XHTML Strict, where such alterations break the standards-compliance of the markup. Fortunately use of Dreamweaver templates stops users from being able to alter this information, and use of stylesheets will automatically override `<body>` link colors.

One additional problem is that contributors can override any individual link's color, even when font alteration is turned off in the administrative settings. They can also use an inline style from an existing stylesheet to override link colors, if there is a suitable class that affects text color. Avoiding these problems should be a part of training users, and included in your style guide.

Advanced Link Properties

Beside the ability to add or edit simple links, Contribute provides a bit more functionality for content editors. These additional advanced link properties are revealed under the *Advanced* button at the bottom of the *Link Properties* panel (*Format > Link Properties*). Contribute provides three additional linking options: creating section anchors, setting target windows and frames, and directly editing the URL (via a different box.)

Creating Section Anchors

Creating a new section anchor is even easier and quicker than creating a regular link; simply choose *Insert > Insert Section Anchor* and type the section anchor name.

An anchor in Contribute's editing window

After a section anchor is created the anchor icon appears; it looks like a little flag (as shown above). Be aware that section anchors will not display if the *Invisible Elements* option in the *Preferences* is disabled. When section anchors already exist on the current page or the page you plan to link to, it is a trivial task to add a new link to a specific anchor. To link to an anchor, simply add or edit a link, specify the page in the main link input line, and then choose the section anchor from the drop-down menu provided in the link panel.

The underlying code produced by this operation will be similar to the following:

```
<a href="#section1"></a>
```

Contribute uses the somewhat aged method of identifying links with the `name` attribute of the `<a>` tag, rather than the more semantically correct method of using the ID attribute inside the `<a>` tag, or any other tag for that matter. (Using the ID attribute allows you to identify more than just a section; it could identify an image, a table, or any other object in the markup.)

Setting Targets and Frames

Contribute handles frames in a similar manner to how it handles targets. While editing a particular frame in a frameset and creating a link, the target drop-down menu will contain all the possible target windows of the frameset, one for each frame (which hopefully have been named properly for easy identification). You must first choose the page you want to link to, and then choose which frame it is to be targeted for. The target option labeled *Entire* page is also useful; it is the same as `target="_top"`, meaning that the linked page will "break out" of the frameset and fill the entire window. If you choose the option labeled *New window* your linked page will open in an entirely new window (your frames will remain intact in the current window). This option uses the `_blank` value for the `target=""` attribute in the link element. Of course, `mailto:` links do not require a target because they are handled uniquely by the browser, opening in the default e-mail application of the web surfer.

Working with Images

Contribute's image capabilities are simple and straightforward. Content contributors can add images to a web page from their local drives or choose an image from the web server. Most of the problems that can arise with images, therefore, may not be directly related to Contribute, but rather to the content contributor's lack of knowledge about image manipulation. We'll get to those points a little later. First, we'll discuss how Contribute handles image files.

Adding New Images or Linking to Existing Ones

Adding an image is completely straightforward and should pose no problems for you or your content editors. Simply drag and drop your image into place and you're done! You can also use *Insert > Image from Website* or *Insert > Image from My Computer*. These options work the same as regular links: you browse through the web server or your local drives (with a thumbnail preview box as an aid) and choose the required image.

Images Types Contribute Handles

Contribute handles all the basic formats commonly used on the Web, but it does not perform conversions or optimization when it imports the image like some professional HTML-editing applications; nor does it integrate with other graphics-editing applications. You should expect that some content contributors will not be versed in image editing and you may encounter odd questions when an editor tries to upload a non-web-friendly image format. Below is a table of common image types, Contribute's support for them, and what Contribute does when it encounters each type. If you expect your users to be handling images often, it would be wise to train them with an image editing application to prepare images correctly for the Web.

File Type	Insert?	Drag-and-drop?
.gif	Yes	Yes
.jpg	Yes	Yes
.png	Yes	Yes
.bmp	Will insert as broken image icon, but image only visible in Windows browsers (uploads to /documents)	Creates link to file(uploads to /documents)
.tif	Will insert as broken image icon, but becomes broken image in browser (uploads to /documents)	Creates link to file(uploads to /documents)
.psd	Will insert as broken image icon, but becomes broken image in browser (uploads to /documents)	Creates link to file(uploads to /documents)

Because of the way Contribute handles these file formats, training of users may be necessary to make sure that they are using the correct format for the correct purpose.

Image Properties and Pitfalls

Take a look at the adjacent screenshot. You will see this dialog box if you double-click on an image in Contribute, or if you select an image and choose *Format > Image Properties*. Though these properties seem self-explanatory, there are hidden factors to consider that are probably not well known to novice graphics editors. To help with this challenge, here are a few important words of advice that need to be impressed upon content editors who use images with Contribute. For more on training your users see *Chapter 6*.

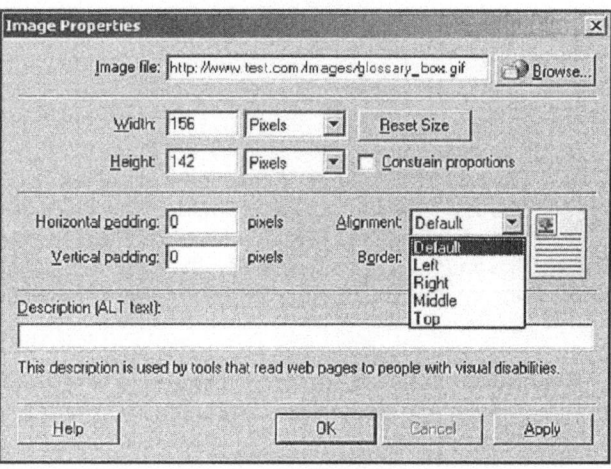

The image properties dialog

Resizing

You should stress to your users that they should rarely resize an image in Contribute. Besides distorting the image, resizing can also make the page load slower because of the browser's need to re-render the image at the new size. Instead, train them to use an image editor (or a friendly graphics expert, perhaps yourself!) to resize the image, and then replace the image in Contribute before publishing the page.

Image File Sizes

Contribute helps to address the issue of image size. Novice Contribute users are unlikely to know that images must be highly optimized for efficient use on the Web. That's why Contribute offers an administrative setting to limit image uploads, of course just because an image is smaller than a set file size, it doesn't mean it's properly optimized.

Image Alignment

Aligning images correctly is not just a Contribute problem, it's an HTML problem. For instance, a user, unless they have text-only editing privileges, can set an image to align to the left, right, middle, or top. This basic browser implementation, though, has never been adequate. Look at the next figure where an image is aligned left in a very common placement.

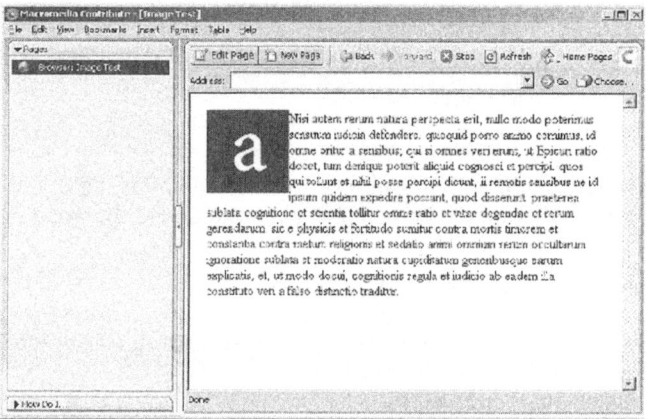

An aligned image with no padding

To the untrained eye, it may seem acceptable, but why is there no padding between the image and the text? Doesn't it look cramped? But there is the handy horizontal padding option that you can set, right? Wrong. Both the horizontal and vertical padding settings add space to opposite sides of the image, not just one side—the right side, where we need it. Were you to add horizontal padding, the image would look a bit better, but still unacceptable, since it would no longer be flush with the left margin.

If you can dissuade your users from using the image align attributes, there are three possible solutions to the image padding problem with Contribute:

- Use a table for image placement (something non-savvy editors may have trouble understanding, and which does not lead to standards-compliant code)

- Manually add padding to the image by editing it in a graphics application like Fireworks or Photoshop (though you will need to train users to do this)

- Use a CSS style for images as shown below (inline images are floated to the left)

```
img { float: left; margin-right: 12px; }
```

This third option is possibly the best currently and could be better in the future if Contribute were to add support for directly applying styles to an image (so not all images would have to be styled in the same manner) *and* browser support for the CSS2 `float` option were more uniformly implemented. At least the CSS option cannot be overridden if the content editor sets an image alignment attribute in the HTML. Ultimately, this problem will require a decision by the web developer about how best to handle image alignment, as well as some training for end users in implementing that solution.

Training Users in Image Preparation

If you have the opportunity, you can train your content editors in the basics of preparing images. It is not likely that you will have a person who is specifically trained and hired to create, locate, and prepare graphics for your site. You may need to rely on content contributors to do this job. At a minimum this is what they should be told:

- Don't use a photo directly out of the digital camera or scanner. A photograph needs to be properly sized and optimized for the Web in an external image-editing application like Photoshop or Fireworks before even launching Contribute. If these tools are not available or are too expensive to purchase, I recommend the thrifty but excellent Adobe Photoshop Elements (US$99) to do basic image preparation work. It has many of the features of the industry-standard Photoshop but is especially tailored for novice users. If a content editor or someone else has the skills, they might want to do some color-correcting as well

- Crop your image so that it is the smallest size possible while still having a reasonable impact. (And then add proper padding if necessary.) This is a balancing act that will improve with time as the content editor becomes more familiar with photo editing and using an image-editing application. Add padding manually if necessary, as the last step before exporting the image for web use

- Optimize your image so that it is the smallest file size possible with the highest quality. This is yet another balancing act that will improve with growing familiarity with your image-editing application's web export features

- Learn when to use GIFs and JPGs. In short, GIF is for very small graphics, icons, line art, logos, and illustrations; JPG is for photos or other graphics with lots of gradations in color or shade. Sometimes experimenting and using your eye is the best way of deciding the better format to use

If All Else Fails...

Remember that there is an option in the administrative settings that will limit content contributors to text-only editing. If you have serious problems maintaining quality or encounter other problems related to design or code, or if you don't need content contributors to deal with images, this is an important option to consider.

Working with Non-HTML Documents

One important feature of Contribute is the facility to import Microsoft Word and Excel files. Before trying to use this feature, you will need to have Microsoft Office (or those particular applications) installed on your PC for Contribute to convert the file. If you don't, Contribute will gray out the option in the *Insert* menu. If you have been sent a Word or Excel file but do not have Microsoft's software to open it, you are out of luck unless you have some type of conversion software to extract the content. Of course, even then the content may not be in the same format as the original. At which point you can cut and paste the content into Contribute.

Adding a Word or Excel Document to a Web Page

There are four ways to add a Word document to a web page into Contribute, and each provides about the same results.

Drag and Drop

As you are editing a web page, simply drag and drop the Word or Excel file from your Desktop or from another directory onto the Contribute editing window at the point you wish the content to begin. Contribute will prompt you with the dialog box asking you whether to convert the document into HTML or simply link to the file. Choose *Insert the contents of the document into this page*:

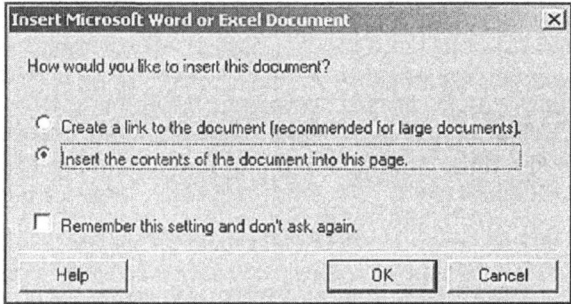

Inserting document contents into a page

Special Note: Macromedia has reported an anomaly that occurs when an Office 97 document is dragged and dropped into Contribute when Office 97 is installed on the user's machine. Since Office 97 doesn't have the ability to copy HTML to the clipboard, Contribute can only import plain text from the file, and all original formatting is lost. To preserve the formatting for Office 97 documents, use the Save As HTML option, and then drag and drop the HTML file into Contribute.

Insert with Menu Command

You can also convert and import documents with a simple menu command: *Insert > Microsoft Word Document* or *Insert > Microsoft Excel Document*. Contribute will prompt with the dialog box mentioned above and complete the conversion.

Cut and Paste (Word)

Cut and paste seems to be a fairly mundane option to explain, but you may encounter some inconsistencies when pasting, usually having to do with paragraph alignment or object placement. If some formatting is lost when you cut and paste a whole Word document or a portion of one, you may not actually be selecting the invisible paragraph markers or other elements in Word that contain the formatting information.

For whole documents, the solution is simple enough: simply use *ctrl-A* (Select All) to select the entire document. This should select all paragraph markers along with all your content.

For portions of documents that you are trying to import, extend the selection past the last character or object to select the closing paragraph marker, which will appear to be an empty space. Macromedia recommends making the invisible formatting elements visible as an aid. To change this preference in Word choose *Tools > Options* and click the *View* tab. Check the All option in the Formatting marks section. This will show all formatting elements and indicate to you where to begin and end your cut and paste operation. Once you understand how the formatting elements work, you can simply turn this option off again.

Link to a File

If you have a Word or Excel file whose content you do not wish to include in the web page itself, you can link directly to the file. Contribute will create the link and upload the file to the appropriate /documents directory when you publish the page.

Microsoft Word Conversion Issues

I don't think any application will ever be able to successfully convert a Word document into HTML while preserving its exact look. HTML, a simple semantic markup language, and Word, a sophisticated word processor with many typographical features not available in HTML, are simply too dissimilar at their core for this to be possible. There is no question there will always be some clean-up necessary after a conversion. Perhaps with time – as CSS matures in its capabilities and browser support grows – there will be a bit more convergence. But even considering this, Contribute still does a pretty good job of at least getting the content into HTML without mangling the code too much. It certainly outperforms some of the professional WYSIWYG editors when it comes to preserving formatting and style from Word documents. It does occasionally leave empty tags, but is generally good about not adding code that is not absolutely necessary. Below are a number of issues to be aware of as you prepare yourself or your editors to import content from Word.

If you know that a Word document will likely be converted to HTML in Contribute, you can teach your users to use Word styles. Structural headers in Word (Header 1, Header 2, and so on) will automatically translate into structural HTML headers in Contribute (`<h1>`, `<h2>`, and so on). Creating a Word template with these styles and training your users to implement them properly is the easiest way to ensure that your Word-to-HTML conversions in Contribute create the cleanest code and the fewest clean-up annoyances.

Links, Images, and non-HTML Documents

Typical issues with Word conversion are shown in the table that follows.

Features marked with an asterisk (*) are discussed in greater detail in the text.		
Feature	**Supported?**	**Comments**
Type sizes		
Type styles		
Bold text	x	Uses `<b>` or `<strong>` as specified in admin settings
Italicized text	x	Uses `<i>` or `<em>` as specified in admin settings
Underlined text	x	Uses `<u>`
Colored text		
Highlighted text		
Header styles (Heading 1, etc.)*	x	Converts to `<h1>`, etc.
Hyperlinks	x	
Paragraph alignment	x	Uses `align`; converts full justify to default alignment
Block style (from style menu)		Converts to default aligned `<p>`
Block indent		Converts to default aligned `<p>`
Bullets	x	Inline bulleting codes correctly; bullets based on styles convert to `&#149;#nbsp;` and do not indent properly
Single line breaks*	x	Converts either to `<p>` or `<p style="margin-top:0;margin-bottom:0">`, depending on admin settings
Special characters*	x	Does not properly convert to HTML 4.01 entities
Table conversion*	x	Cell padding and spacing must be re-set
Table alignment	x	Uses `align`; surrounds table with `<div>`
Table borders		
Table cell shading	x	Uses `bgcolor`
Table cell alignment	x	Uses `align` or `valign`
Table merged cells	x	Uses `colspan` or `rowspan`
Table empty cells	x	Does not add ` ` or spacers
Graphics	x	Places image in its own `<p>`; does not handle padding or text wrapping
Text boxes		Puts content in `<p>`; may add an extra `<p>` before the containing `<p>`
Tabs	x	Converts to two non-breaking spaces (`  `)
Two consecutive spaces		Remains in HTML markup, but not coded as entities (even when consecutive spaces option is enabled in admin settings)
Small caps (and other special text styles)		Reverts to normal text
Drop caps		Drop cap becomes plain letter inside a single-celled table; text resumes in a new `<p>`

Converting Paragraphs and Line Breaks

Contribute has an administrative setting that requires you to decide how Contribute's markup will handle line breaks, both in the Contribute editing window and when converting Word to HTML. Let's review those options and their implications for Word document conversion:

The *one line* setting uses inline CSS styling to simulate a word processor line break – similar to a `<br />` Typical code looks like this:

```
<p style="margin-top:0;margin-bottom:0;">content</p>
```

There is potential for disaster when using this setting if your Word document uses paragraph formatting that adds space before or after a paragraph (Format > Paragraph > Spacing) rather than two line breaks, which is the typical case. In the first case, there will be no spacing between paragraphs at all. For a long document, this could be tedious to clean up. In the second case, Contribute recognizes that two line breaks equal a new paragraph and thus starts a new paragraph (`<p>`) without inline styling (thereby adding space between paragraphs).

The *two lines* setting creates simple `<p>` markup without inline styles:

```
<p>content</p>
```

Like the *one line* setting, each line break starts a new paragraph. This setting would not work well for Word documents with lots of lists or items separated by a single line break, since this would create space between all of them, as demonstrated in the diagram below.

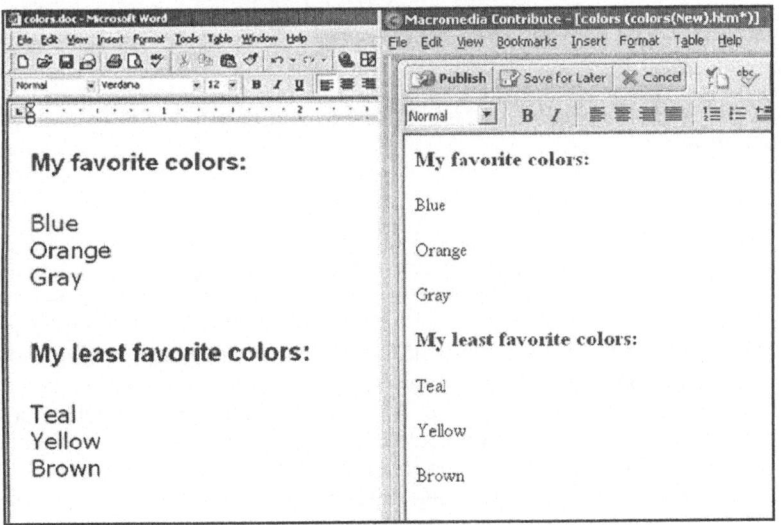

How spacing can change from Word to Contribute

In general the best option for maximizing conversion effectiveness and minimizing text clean-up would be the *two lines* setting. It is easy enough for the Contribute editor to use *Shift + Return* for a single line break in those instances where it is needed. Contribute will insert a `<br />`.

If you use `<br />` exclusively for spacing, to the exclusion of `<p>`, perhaps it is time that you begin to wean yourself off that habit. Beside the fact that it will be virtually impossible to use Contribute if you demand `<br />`s in your markup, there is another good reason — the World Wide Web Consortium (W3C) is poised to deprecate the `<br />` tag in XHTML 2.0.

Alignment Handling

For the most part, when converting from Word, Contribute handles alignment well for most blocks of text, tables, and objects. Contribute aligns text or objects by using the align attribute inside either a `<p>` or a `<div>`.

If you prefer to fully-justify your text, that formatting will be lost, as it has no equivalent in straight HTML. You could, however, create a CSS style to allow your users to full-justify a paragraph. Of course, you will need to provide your users with a helpful CSS style guide.

Style and Font Issues

There are a few points to make about how Contribute handles text styling when converting a Word document:

- Fonts specified in Word are not preserved in the markup. For coders who use stylesheets exclusively, this is good news. Remember to turn off the `<font>` capabilities in the administrative settings if you want to enforce your styles.

- Text styled with a header style (under the *Style* menu in Word) will instead be styled with the corresponding `<hn>` tag.

- Font sizing is not preserved when importing. Text reverts to the default HTML size (size 3 in most browsers).

Special Characters

One apparent oversight in the Word conversion capability is the markup of special characters such as copyright (©), em dashes (—), and the trademark symbol (™). When these characters are added to the web page through Contribute (Insert > Special Characters), the underlying markup correctly uses character entities from the Latin-1 (ISO-8859-1) or Unicode character sets adopted by the HTML 4.01 specification. But when importing from Word, these same characters are not encoded at all, and are placed directly into the markup. This doesn't seem to be a problem for modern browsers, but it's not a good markup practice and could cause text gremlins in certain situations. See the table that follows for a representative set of the most common special characters to watch out for, along with their corresponding Latin-1 or Unicode entities.

Character Name	Symbol	HTML 4.01 Entity
Em dash	—	— or —
En dash	–	– or –
Ampersand	&	& or &
Trademark symbol	™	™ or ™
Registered trademark symbol	®	® or ®
Copyright symbol	©	© or ©
Ellipsis	…	… or &hellep;
Left single quotation mark	'	‘ or ‘
Right single quotation mark	'	’ or ’
Left double quotation mark	"	“ or “
Right double quotation mark	"	” or ”
Pound symbol	£	£ or £
Euro symbol	€	€ or €

Tables

The only drawback about Contribute's table conversion from Word is that borders and grids are not preserved. This is somewhat understandable, since it has never been easy to create tables in HTML with borders on only certain cells, rows, or columns (for instance, a thick outer border with a hairline cell grid).

The good news is that overall table positioning is preserved, as well as background colors and intra-cell alignments. Column widths default to percentages, calculated from the size the table appears in Word.

Graphics

Graphics that are inserted into the body of a Word document are transferred to the web page as GIFs or JPGs at the size they appear in the Word document, even if they were originally different sizes and were modified in Word. Contribute will preserve the original filename of each image if you named it before it was placed inside the Word document. Contribute re-samples Word- and Excel-embedded images to 96 ppi instead of the more common 72 ppi for web graphics, something that might slightly affect the look of your site, but since monitor resolutions have been steadily increasing this is fairly reasonable. (Other images added directly to a page retain their original parameters.)

For images that were originally imported into Word or Excel, Contribute decides which image format to use based on the original image. If the original embedded image is an 8-bit/indexed color image (for example BMP, GIF, or 8-bit PNG), Contribute will create a GIF. If the original image is a JPEG, or some other 24-bit image, Contribute will use the JPEG format. Contribute does not create PNG files from embedded images in Word or Excel.

Other Markup Problems and Limitations

As with any WYSIWYG markup application, there are always at least minor problems with markup, but Contribute generates surprisingly few errors in its Word conversion algorithm. In places where there are several line breaks, Contribute may throw in an extra pair of paragraph tags. In some instances text or objects may be placed between <div> tags for no apparent reason. And in at least one instance (where a textbox was used) there was an extra <p> tag with no closing tag – the only instance where I saw markup that did not validate to basic HTML markup specifications.

3

Links, Images, and non-HTML Documents

Macromedia also established an import file size limit of 300K for Word and Excel documents, something you will want to make your users aware of. If your users need to import a large document, they may consider breaking it up into smaller segments and publishing them as linked pages. This is a more web-savvy practice anyway. Contribute will remind you of this with an error message if you try to import a 300K+ document.

What to Do When Converting Word Documents

So how should you or your content contributors prepare Word documents for conversion, and what things will you need to clean up afterwards? Here is a simple checklist of the important points just covered that will lead to better code and a happier site administrator:

Before Converting

- Simplify the document by removing textboxes, drop caps, extraneous graphics, or anything you know will not translate properly into HTML

- Make the document more self describing: use the style menu to create and apply styles for main headings, subheadings, and section headings. Contribute's markup will be much cleaner and more professional

- Take note of fonts, font sizes, font colors, highlights, or special font variants – these will be eliminated automatically. You don't have to remove them, but you might want to replace them once the document is in HTML

- Prepare the document for the Web by creating more concise and succinct content: use bulleted and numbered lists (which translate well and with proper formatting), judicious bolding and italicization where necessary to bring out important points, and break up long stretches of text where necessary to increase readability

After Converting

- If you've imported into a template with stylesheets, there should be little to do if the document was prepared as fully as possible. Extra styling can be achieved through defined classes in the *Style* menu, unless the user is set to text only. In that case, there is no need to worry about much styling anyway

- If the document was imported into a blank document, you can set styles through the *Font* menus. The administrator of the site should train users on adding any styling that may have been removed during conversion (such as what to do with highlights, colored text, and so forth)

- Check for special characters: delete these and add them back using the *Insert > Special Characters* menu

- Check any tables to see if they need slight resizing or alignment adjustments

- Check for other alignment or placement problems, especially with images. Images can be cut and re-pasted within the document if necessary

Microsoft Excel Conversion Issues

Contribute treats Excel files as if they are large tables. Conversion is achieved by starting in the upper-left corner of the spreadsheet and is mapped as a table from that point across and down to the lowermost and rightmost cell that has content. In general, for simple spreadsheets filled with data, Contribute is flawless in its conversion, except that it has some of the same limitations as Word when it comes to borders and colored text. Most Excel conversion problems are the same as those described in the *Special Characters* table earlier in the chapter.

Things begin to get dicey when Contribute encounters an Excel file that has objects (like generated charts) or other embedded images or objects. Excel actually generates charts as image objects (embedded GIF files), so they behave (and convert) similarly to Word's embedded images (see "*Word Conversion Issues: Graphics*" for how Contribute handles embedded images in Word and Excel documents).

Linking To or Importing Other Non-HTML Files

Linking to a non-HTML file that is already on the web server is not a clear option in the *Link Properties* panel, and this is likely to cause confusion and frustration with users. Though it is not at all clear how, you can indeed link to a non-HTML file on the server. You must choose the *Browse to Web Page* link method from the toolbar or under *Format > Link Properties* to modify an existing link. Simply click the *Browse...* button. After the mini-browser appears, there is a button in the upper-right corner labeled *Choose...* (see below). Contribute will present you with a directory listing of your web site for you to choose a file to which to link.

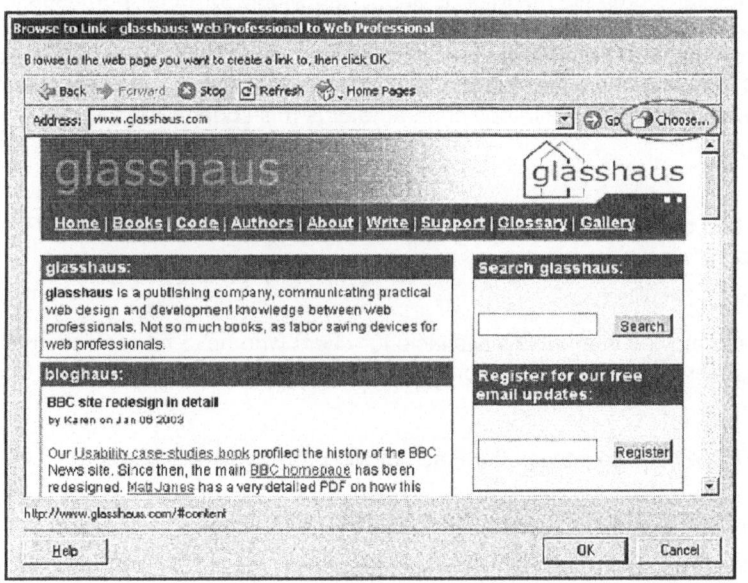

Browse to Web Page dialog showing the Choose button

If someone else besides your Contribute editor is responsible for creating non-HTML documents to be added to your web site, it is a good practice to place these documents in an agreed-upon directory if possible and link to them on the server rather than on your local drives. This will prevent the documents from being scattered among many directories, since Contribute uploads non-HTML files to different /documents directories depending on where the page is being published.

Portable Document Format Documents (PDFs)

PDFs are handled as typical linked files (there is no PDF import function to convert them to HTML). If the PDF is on your local drive, simply drag and drop the file into place to create a link. You can also select *Insert > File on My Computer* to browse your local drives and add the PDF to your page. (Remember that your PDFs will be uploaded to the /documents directory of the directory where your page is being published.)

Flash Objects

Contribute allows content contributors to insert Flash objects (.swf files) when they have full editing privileges. Flash objects are movies, text, or buttons that are originally created in Flash or Dreamweaver.

To insert a Flash object into a web page, click in the desired location to establish an insertion point. Choose *Insert > Flash Movie* and navigate on your local drive to choose the Flash object. You may need to choose *All Files in the Files of Type...* menu to see your .swf files. To choose a Flash movie that is already on your web server, see *Linking or importing other non-HTML files*.

Although drag-and-drop file insertion is supported widely for other purposes in Contribute (adding Word/Excel files, adding images, linking to documents), there are problems with its implementation for Flash objects, and I do not recommend using it. First, despite where you drag the file, it will be inserted at the top of the page. Second, and most disconcerting, the Flash object is not uploaded by Contribute, but rather the Flash object parameter is mis-coded like this:

```
<param name="movie" value="file:///Z|/flashmovie.swf">
```

The published page on the server is erroneously pointing to a directory and file that does not exist on the web server.

Flash Movie Properties

Adding Flash movies is a feature available for users who have no restrictions on editing content. If you give a user or user group text-only editing privileges, they are not able to add or delete Flash movies.

There are three ways to access the Flash movie properties dialog box:

- Double-click the Flash object in the document window
- Select *Format > Flash Movie Properties*, or
- Right-click on the Flash object and select *Flash Movie Properties*

Contribute allows an editor to set only two Flash object properties: *Start playing the movie when the page loads and Loop the movie.* When *Start playing the movie when the page loads* is chosen the Flash movie will begin playing automatically once the page loads in the browser. *Loop the movie* causes the movie to play continuously, regardless of whether the movie has an internal "Stop" action.

Markup

Below is the full markup Contribute writes when inserting a Flash object:

```
<object classid="clsid:D27CDB6E-AE6D-11cf-96B8-444553540000"
codebase="http://download.macromedia.com/pub/shockwave/cabs/flash/swflash.cab#vers
ion=6,0,29,0" width="700" height="500">
<param name="movie" value="documents/flashmovie.swf">
<param name="loop" value="false">
<param name="quality" value="high">
<embed src="documents/flashmovie.swf" quality="high"
pluginspage="http://www.macromedia.com/go/getflashplayer" type="application/x-
shockwave-flash" width="700" height="500"></embed>
</object>
```

If you have Flash movies with special parameters that need to be set, you will have to manually modify this code and lock it in a template or locked region

Note that Contribute includes the deprecated `<embed>` tag for compatibility with older browsers, including all pre-version 6 Netscape browsers, even when using a XHTML Strict DOCTYPE, where technically this tag is not allowed.

Resizing

Contribute users can change the size of a Flash movie by selecting it and dragging the resize handles. If your Flash movie contains bitmapped images, this could create a problem with distortion. If you use Flash movies as part of a page, and it is important they do not become distorted, then it is best to put them in a locked area of a template.

Text and Rich Text Files

There are three options for using plain text files and rich text files (`.txt` and `.rtf`) in Contribute. You can create a standard link to the file (see "*Linking or importing other non-HTML files*" earlier). This will add only a link to your page, not the content. Alternatively, you can perform a simple cut and paste of the document's content. Lastly, you can import the document's content by using the *Insert > Microsoft Word Document function*. Note, however that this feature is dependent on having Microsoft Office installed on your system. If you can't import Word documents, you can't use this feature for text files either. In the case of `.rtf` files, using this option will preserve most, if not all, the document's formatting.

3

Links, Images, and non-HTML Documents

PowerPoint Presentations

Microsoft PowerPoint files can be added to your web page as a link, just as we've seen previously with other non-HTML files. Depending on your target audience's capabilities, it may be best to compress (zip) the file to force a download of the PowerPoint file when a user clicks on the link. If you know that your target audience is likely to have PowerPoint, Internet Explorer with the PowerPoint Active X control activated, or a PowerPoint viewer plugin installed, you may not need to do this. One thing you *will* need to do is ensure that your web server recognizes the MIME type of your non-HTML files (whether .ppt, .pps, .zip, or any other file type. If you do not have access to your web server configuration settings, consult your web hosting provider for support).

If you've used the web export function to make your PowerPoint more accessible, you will see that PowerPoint exports many HTML files and (rather large) GIFs. You must be sure to link to the parent frameset HTML page that contains links to all the resources needed to display the presentation. Upon uploading this page, Contribute will upload all the dependent files as well.

There are also great tools available to convert a PowerPoint presentation into a Flash (SWF) movie, something Contribute will handle well. One such excellent tool is PowerCONVERTER created by PresentationPRO (*www.presentationpro.com*). Within seconds a PowerPoint file can be converted to a .swf file, ready for adding to your web site through Contribute. However, while useful, this tool will add another expense and users will need training to use it.

If you plan to allow your users to upload non-HTML files to the server and you'd like for the files to be automatically opened in particular applications or with certain plugins, you will need to ensure that your web server recognizes their MIME types. For instance, a typical Apache web server has a MIME type recognition file (named mime.types*) with lines like this:*

```
application/powerpoint          ppt pps
```

This line tells the server that any file with an extension of .ppt *or* .pps *corresponds to the MIME-type* application/powerpoint *and should be handled with Powerpoint. This will in turn assist a visitor's browser in figuring out what to do with the file. The browser will look for the helper application or a suitable plug-in, or (if all else fails) simply offer to download the file. If you do not have access to your web server configuration settings, consult your web hosting provider for support).*

Audio/Video Media Files

There is no support for adding or editing multimedia files, though this doesn't preclude your users from adding to your site them simply as files. Both QuickTime and Windows Media audio files and movies can be directly linked using the standard HTTP protocol. The media files will be downloaded as the user waits. QuickTime, since it has a "progressive download" feature, will actually begin playing in the browser before the full download has finished, mimicking more sophisticated streaming media content. Windows Media files will launch the Windows Media player installed on all Windows installations when the download has completed.

Summary

Though there are some controls in Contribute's administrative settings to limit what the content editor can do on any given web page, this chapter has covered things that a user can do when most or all of the controls are relaxed:

- Adding links

- Adding, placing, and modifying images

- Adding content from other documents, and styling that content

You'll also have gleaned tips and tactics for helping these content editors contribute in a meaningful way, hopefully without wreaking havoc on the underlying markup.

As a web developer and the administrator of a site, you will be responsible for determining what tolerance level you or your organization has for allowing content editors to have influence on design aspects of the web site in addition to the content they are creating and editing. Even if you need to provide maximum flexibility and freedom to your editors, you now have a few ideas at your disposal to help you manage the content contribution process.

4

In this Chapter

- Modifying the Contribute Welcome page

- Modifying the How Do I... panel

- Contribute preferences

- Customizing user groups

- Inherited Dreamweaver MX extensibility

Author: Lyn Wall

Customizing Contribute

Contribute enables you to tailor key components to the specific needs of your users. You can create a personalized experience that will make your users feel more comfortable, and provide customized instructions, helping to minimize the time you need to spend on direct support. Customization also facilitates the enforcement of design standards and the best practices discussed in *Chapter 5*.

In this chapter, we will discuss:

- Modifying the Contribute Welcome page your users see when they launch Contribute
- Modifying the How Do I panel by adding and removing sections to meet your organization's needs
- Extending the Contribute interface by setting permissions and defaults for new and existing pages
- Taking advantage of inherited Dreamweaver MX extensibility

You will also find a very useful PDF called *Extending Contribute* available for download from *http://www.macromedia.com/support/contribute/extend.html*.

Skills

At a minimum, you should have a thorough understanding of HTML, and the ability to read and interpret code, in order to successfully customize any aspect of Contribute. Each aspect of customization requires its own set of skills.

The Welcome Page

You should have a thorough familiarity with HTML code in order to update the Welcome page. Although it is possible to modify this page with a WYSIWIG editor, you should be able to read the code behind the page well enough to understand Dreamweaver MX template tags.

The How Do I Panel

It is best to have a good understanding of how custom tags are used and defined in XML. You will not need to create tags or document definitions, but you need to be able to modify the code in several XML files. You will also need to be able to create HTML documents. For more complex implementations, you should have a thorough understanding of JavaScript and be able to write code with JavaScript API calls.

Inherited Dreamweaver Extensibility

This is an advanced function that should be attempted only if you have experience with Dreamweaver's extensibility features.

The Configuration Folder

All of the files we will discuss modifying in this chapter are located in the `Configuration` folder of the Contribute program directory, typically `C:\Program Files\Macromedia\Contribute\Configuration` on Windows PCs. However, you could install the Contribute directory anywhere, so we will use `%CONTRIBUTE%` to generically refer to the path to the `Contribute` folder (that is, it would represent `C:\Program Files\Macromedia\Contribute` in the typical path above.)

It is strongly recommended you make a copy of this entire folder and place it in a different directory. This way, if you have any problems with the files you modify, you will have a backup available. It's also good practice to test your changes after modifying each file – this way you will be able to know exactly which file is causing the problem, cutting down on troubleshooting time.

Modifying the Contribute Welcome Page

By customizing the start page, you can make your Contribute users feel even more comfortable by giving them a familiar environment with easily available guidance geared to their needs. After connecting to our sample site, the default Welcome page will look like this:

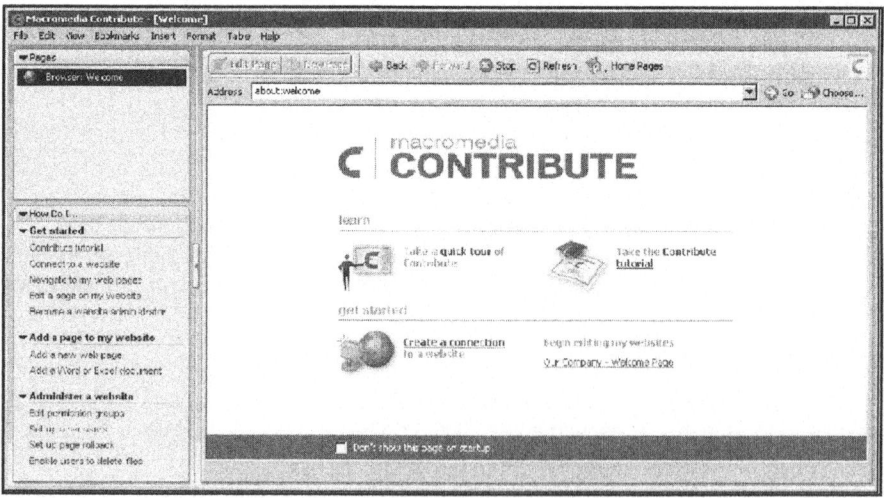

The Contribute welcome screen, after a connection has been made.

This is a good start, but we can improve on it by modifying it with our users in mind. You can add your company or customer's logo, as well as links to tasks specific to your site.

Creating a New Welcome Page

When Contribute is launched, it automatically creates and displays an HTML page based on the `welcome.dwt` template, located in the `%CONTRIBUTE%\Configuration\Content\Welcome` folder of the Contribute program directory. We're going to create a new Welcome page for our sample web site by making changes to this template.

Below, we will discuss all the changes we need to make to the default welcome template to create our new Welcome page. You can also find our new `welcome.dwt` template file in the code download for this chapter, available from *http://www.glasshaus.com*.

This section assumes a basic knowledge of Dreamweaver MX Templates. If you do not have this knowledge, read up on templates in *Chapter 7* – you must be careful not to change any of the code that controls the template.

Changing the Template

We're going to replace the Contribute logo with our sample site's logo; then we will move the link to create a connection and the list of sites to be the first thing on the page. We'll also make some changes to the styles in the `<head>` section of the template, to customize the colors and fonts. So, load up `welcome.dwt` in your favorite editor:

The style section of the default page looks like this:

```
<style type="text/css">
  <!--
    a:visited {
      color: #0000FF;
    }
    a:hover {
      text-decoration: none;
    }
    body {
      margin-top: 15px;
      margin-left: 15px;
      background-color: #FFFFFF;
    }
    .label {
      font: bold 11px Tahoma, Verdana, Arial, Helvetica, sans-serif;
      color: #999999;
    }
    .welcomeItems {
      font: 11px/18px Tahoma, Verdana, Arial, Helvetica, sans-serif;
    }
  -->
</style>
```

We'll make some changes to match the sample site. We'll change the link and background color to match the colors on our sample site (as defined in CSS/basic.css – see the sample site in the code download for this chapter).

We want all links to have the same appearance on the new Welcome page, regardless of whether or not they have been visited before, so we will add the a:link selector after the a:visited selector in our stylesheet. We will also change the color to match the sample site, specify the font-family with alternatives in case the user does not have the exact font on their machine, and set the font-weight to bold.

To be consistent with the style for the <body> tag, we also want to define the default paragraph style for the <p> tag, so we'll add the p selector after the body selector in our CSS. Next, we'll change the background color to match the background on our sample site, and define the default font family, size, and color.

The font family and color of the <h1> tag will be the same, so we'll also add the h1 selector to the style section and define the color and font-family.

Finally, we want the lines on the page to be the same color as the text, so we add the <hr> selector to the style section and define the color to match the text.

After all our changes have been made, the style section in the head of our document should now look like this:

```
<style type="text/css">
  <!--
    a:visited, a:link {
      color: #000099;
      font-family: Arial, Helvetica, sans-serif;
      font-weight: bold;
    }
    a:hover {
      text-decoration: none;
    }
    body, p {
      margin-top: 15px;
      margin-left: 15px;
      background-color: #f4f0e4;
      color: #666666;
      font-family: Arial, Helvetica, sans-serif;
      font-size: 10pt;
    }
    .label {
      font: bold 11px Verdana, Arial, Helvetica, sans-serif;
      color: #666666;
    }
    .welcomeItems {
      font: 11px/18px Tahoma, Verdana, Arial, Helvetica, sans-serif;
    }
    h1 {
      font-family: Arial, Helvetica, sans-serif;
      color: #000099;
    }
```

```
  hr {
    color: #000099
  }
 -->
</style>
```

The changes made to the rest of the template file are as follows:

This is the original `<table>` definition tag:

```
<table bgcolor="#ffffff" border="0" cellpadding="0" cellspacing="0" width="456"
     align="center">
```

We will change the background color of the main table to match the background color we set in our style section, and change the width of the table from 456px to 88%:

```
<table bgcolor="#f4f0e4" border="0" cellpadding="0" cellspacing="0" width="88%"
     align="center">
```

We will also replace the Macromedia Contribute logo with the logo for Our Company, changing:

```
<img name="welcome_r1_c1" src="Assets/welcome_r1_c1.jpg" width="456" height="87"
     border="0" alt="Macromedia Contribute logo">
```

to

```
<img src="Assets/head.gif" alt="Our Company logo" name="welcome_r1_c1" width="528"
     height="74" border="0" align="right">
```

We will assume that the users have already been given an introductory course in Contribute and therefore just want to get started, so we've moved the connection information to the top row:

```
<tr>
  <td colspan="4" valign="top">
    <hr />    <h1>Welcome! </h1>
    <p>Here you will be able to make changes to the site in a familiar
environment. </p>
    <p>If this is your first time here, please click below to initialize a
connection with
    the site.<br />
      <a href="mm:createSite" target="_top">Create a connection</a>
    </p>
    <p>If you already have a connection, click below to begin editing:<br />
      <!-- TemplateBeginIf cond="HasSites" -->
      <!-- TemplateBeginRepeat name="Site" -->
      <!-- TemplateBeginEditable name="SiteName" -->
      <a href="#">Site name</a><!-- TemplateEndEditable --><br />
      <!-- TemplateEndRepeat --><!-- TemplateEndIf -->
    </p>
  </td>
  <td> </td>
</tr>
```

We have also modified the learning section to match the style of Our Company, changing

```
<tr>
   <td width="75" valign="middle" class="label">
     <img src="Assets/welcome_r3_c1.jpg" alt="Take a quick tour of Contribute"
          name="welcome_r3_c1" width="75" height="68" border="0" align="left"
          usemap="#welcome_r3_c1Map">
   </td>
   <td valign="top" class="label"><br />
     Take a
     <a href="http://www.macromedia.com/go/see_contribute" target="_top">quick
tour</a>
     of Contribute
   </td>
   <td width="70" valign="middle" class="label">
     <img src="Assets/welcome_r3_c2.jpg" alt="Take the Contribute tutorial"
          name="welcome_r3_c2" width="75" height="68"
          border="0" align="left" usemap="#welcome_r3_c2Map">
   </td>
   <td valign="top" class="label"><br />
       Take the <a href="mm:tutorial" target="_top">Contribute tutorial</a>
   </td>
   <td>
     <img src="Assets/spacer.gif" width="1" height="68" border="0" alt="">
   </td>
</tr>
```

to

```
<table bgcolor="#f4f0e4" border="0" cellpadding="0" cellspacing="0"
       width="88%" align="center">
   <!-- fwtable fwsrc="CON_welcome_screen_sliced.png" fwbase="welcome.jpg"
        fwstyle="Dreamweaver" fwdocid = "742308039" fwnested="0" -->
   <tr>
     <td colspan="2">
       <img src="Assets/spacer.gif" width="237" height="1" border="0" alt="">
     </td>
     <td colspan="2">
       <img src="Assets/spacer.gif" width="219" height="1" border="0" alt="">
     </td>
     <td width="0%">
       <img src="Assets/spacer.gif" width="1" height="1" border="0" alt="">
     </td>
   </tr>
   <tr>
     <td colspan="4" valign="top">
       <img src="Assets/head.gif" alt="Our Company logo" name="welcome_r1_c1"
            width="528" height="74" border="0" align="right">
     </td>
     <td>
       <img src="Assets/spacer.gif" width="1" height="87" border="0" alt="">
     </td>
   </tr>
   <tr>
     <td colspan="4" valign="top">
```

```
    <hr /><h1>Welcome! </h1>
    <p>
       Here you will be able to make changes to the site in a familiar
environment.
    </p>
    <p>
       If this is your first time here, please click below to initialize a
       connection with the site.<br />
       <a href="mm:createSite" target="_top">Create a connection</a>
    </p>
    <p>
       If you already have a connection, click below to begin editing:<br />
       <!-- TemplateBeginIf cond="HasSites" -->
       <!-- TemplateBeginRepeat name="Site" -->
       <!-- TemplateBeginEditable name="SiteName" -->
       <a href="#">Site name</a>
       <!-- TemplateEndEditable --><br />
       <!-- TemplateEndRepeat -->
       <!-- TemplateEndIf -->
    </p>
  </td>
  <td> </td>
</tr>
<tr>
  <td colspan="4" valign="top">
    <hr /><h2>Would you like to learn more about Contribute?</h2>
  </td>
  <td>
    <img src="Assets/spacer.gif" width="1" height="40" border="0" alt="">
  </td>
</tr>
<tr>
  <td width="14%" valign="middle" class="label">
    <img src="Assets/welcome_r3_c1.jpg" alt="Take a quick tour of Contribute"
         name="welcome_r3_c1" width="75" height="68" border="0" align="left"
         usemap="#welcome_r3_c1Map">
  </td>
  <td width="35%" valign="top" class="label"><br />
    Take a
    <a href="http://www.macromedia.com/go/see_contribute" target="_top">quick
tour</a>
    of Contribute.
  </td>
  <td width="13%" valign="middle" class="label">
    <img src="Assets/welcome_r3_c2.jpg" alt="Take the Contribute tutorial"
         name="welcome_r3_c2" width="75" height="68" border="0" align="left"
         usemap="#welcome_r3_c2Map">
  </td>
  <td width="38%" valign="top" class="label"><br />
    Take the <a href="mm:tutorial" target="_top">Contribute tutorial</a>
  </td>
  <td>
    <img src="Assets/spacer.gif" width="1" height="68" border="0" alt="">
  </td>
</tr>
</table>
```

We then added a link to follow for support when using Contribute:

```
<tr>
  <td colspan="4" rowspan="2" valign="top" class="label">
    <hr />
    <p style="text-align: center">
      If you need additional assistance, please contact
      <a href="support@ourcompany.com">support@ourcompany.com</a><br />
      or call extension 5555
    </p>
  </td>
  <td>
    <img src="Assets/spacer.gif" width="1" height="32" border="0" alt="">
  </td>
</tr>
<tr>
  <td><img src="Assets/spacer.gif" width="1" height="28" border="0" alt=""></td>
</tr>
```

Our new welcome page will look like this when Contribute is opened:

I used Fireworks MX to change the background color of the Contribute Quick Tour and Tutorial icons.

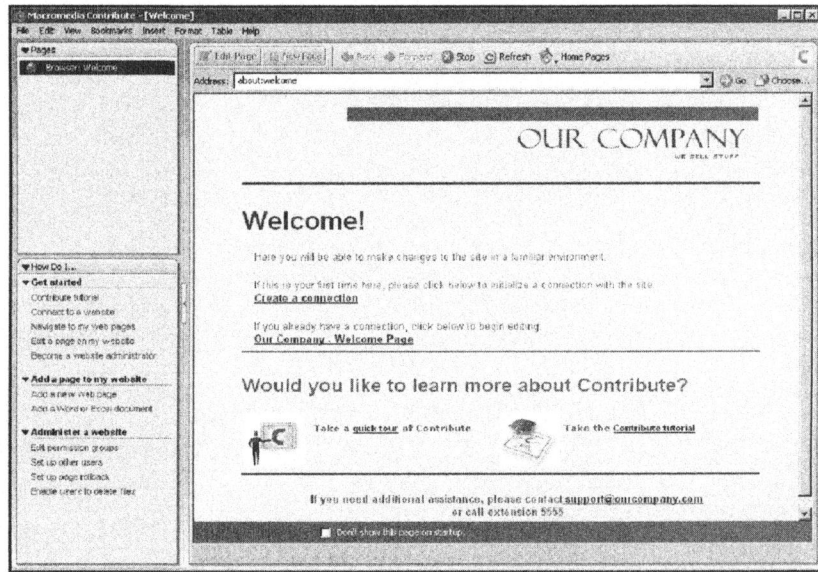

Our new modified welcome screen.

Delivering the New Welcome Page

To deliver the new start page to your users, you must replace the old `welcome.dwt` with the new version `welcome.dwt` in each user's `Welcome` folder. Place any images you modified or added to the Welcome page in the `Welcome\Assets` folder. This could be done manually by using a self-extracting zip file that unzips to a specific location, or you could create a custom installation file for the necessary files.

The updated versions are included in the code download for this book, along with our company logo, and the updated template file.

Modifying the "How Do I..." Section

Your users' needs are unique to your site and their workgroup. Contribute enables you to add instructions to the *How Do I...* panel that will give additional guidance specific to the people working on your site. For instance, if you know that your users will be adding content to a calendar section, you may want to write instructions that specify the name of the page to update, and anything specific about how to format the calendar entry. Your users will feel more comfortable and you'll receive even fewer support calls!

The *How Do I...* section is written using XML, but don't worry, you don't need to be an XML expert to modify this section, because the elements and documents are already set up. If you want to add a document, you can copy and modify an existing document. If you understand how XML is used to create custom element definitions, you should feel comfortable editing the task section as long as you carefully adhere to the syntax for each element.

There are three primary files that control the *How Do I...*panel:

- `Tasks.xml` defines the tasks listed in the main menu
- `TasksLayout.xml` sets the spacing of the tasks within the panel
- `Tasks.css` is the stylesheet that defines the appearance of the panel

Additionally, each individual task is defined by its own HTML file. You can assign the name of each task's file individually.

The Default How Do I... panel.

Customizing Contribute

Tasks.xml

The *How Do I...* section is defined by `tasks.xml`, which is located in Contribute's `Configuration\Content\Tasks` directory, and contains all the content of the *How Do I...* panel. This file defines the XML elements that the panel uses to display a list of instructions and links to HTML documents with the instructions to be displayed. These are three elements you will need to understand:

- `<tasks>`: This is the top-level element in the element hierarchy for the `Tasks.xml` file

- `<category>`: These elements are the only children of the `<tasks>` element, that is, they are the only element type that is directly below `<tasks>` in the hierarchy. Each `<category>` element contains the information for an entire subsection of the *How Do I...* panel, for example, *Get Started*

- `<task />`: These are empty elements (that is, elements that don't contain any child elements) that are the only children of the `<category>` elements. Each `<task />` element contains the information for one specific item within a *How Do I...* category, for example, *Become a website administrator*

Here is a sample excerpt from the `Tasks.xml` file, to give you more of an idea of what it looks like:

```xml
<?xml version='1.0' encoding='utf-8'?>
<tasks id="tasks">
  <category name="Get started" id="0">
    <task name="Contribute tutorial " file="task2.htm" id="1"/>
    <task name="Connect to a website" file="task14.htm" id="2"/>
    <task name="Navigate to my web pages" file="task17.htm" id="3"/>
    <task name="Edit a page on my website " file="task18.htm" id="4"/>
    <task name="Become a website administrator" file="task19.htm" id="5"/>
  </category>

  . . .

</tasks>
```

<tasks>

The `<tasks>` element is the top-level tag for the document, similar to the `<html>` element in an HTML document. It contains the categories of tasks that are available. You will never need to make any changes to the `<tasks>` element. The only attribute this element has is `id`, which is required to identify the task as a unique element within the file. For example:

```xml
<tasks id="mytasks">
  . . .
</tasks>
```

\<category\>

The \<category\> element groups a set of tasks together. Each category can be expanded and collapsed in the *How Do I...* panel, and can be enabled or disabled. The possible attributes of the \<category\> element are as follows:

- id (required): Identifies each category – must be unique within the tasks.xml file

- name (required): This is the text displayed as the category title in the *How Do I...* panel, which also provides a link to expand/collapse the category

- enabled (optional): The attribute value is a JavaScript expression that evaluates to True or False, defaulting to True if not specified. When the value is set to True, the task is available to the user; when it is set to False, it is not

- stylecollapsed (optional): If you want to specify a custom style for the category name when it is collapsed, you can specify it using the stylecollapsed attribute. Note that the attribute value must be the name of a style defined in the tasks.css file. The default style is clsCategoryCollapsed

- styleexpanded (optional): If you want to specify a custom style for the category name when it is expanded, you can specify it using the styleexpanded attribute. Note that the attribute value must be the name of a style defined in the tasks.css file. The default style is clsCategoryExpanded

- update (optional): This tells Contribute when to check to see if the category should be enabled (if the enabled attribute should be set to True.) Events that can trigger a check are onWorkspaceChange (occurs when the user switches between Browse and Edit modes), onURLChange (occurs when the user browsers to a different page), onEdit (occurs when the user makes a change to the draft they are working on), onSelChange (occurs when the user changes the selection in the draft page), and onEveryIdle (occurs whenever the contributor is idle). Note that these events are listed in order from least to most processor-intensive

This is the code for the \<category\> element of the default category *Modify a web page* in Contribute's task.xml file. It is enabled when you are editing a web page on your site and disabled when you are in Browse mode:

```
<category name="Modify a web page"
enabled="CCWorkspaceManager.getManager(dw.getDocumentDOM()).getState() == 'edit'"
id="14"> ...
...</category>
```

This looks complicated, but CCWorkspaceManager.getManager(dw.getDocumentDOM()).getState() simply tests to see whether Contribute is in Edit or Browse mode. It makes sense that the task *Modify a web page* would only be enabled when Contribute is in Edit mode.

This code to assign the enabled state of the task is JavaScript that takes advantage of Dreamweaver's Extensibility API. For more information on how to take advantage of the Extensibility API, visit Macromedia Dreamweaver MX Application Development Center at *http://www.macromedia.com/desdev/mx/dreamweaver/*.

4

Customizing Contribute

<task>

The <task> element describes a task you define, and provides a link to a page describing the steps the user needs to take to carry out this task. The attributes of the <task> element are as follows:

- id (required):The id attribute must be unique within all elements in the tasks.xml file

- name (required): This is the text link displayed in the *How Do I...* panel for the task, and acts as a link to the instructions for the task

- command (optional*):This is a string that specifies JavaScript code to run when the user clicks the task name. For instance, clicking a task can open a specific document for editing or display a set of instructions as a task in the *How Do I...* panel

- commandfile (optional*): commandfile names a file that will execute JavaScript. It must include any arguments required by the script. The syntax is: commandfile="'mycommandfile.htm', 'argument1', 'argument2'". It should include as many arguments as are required by the JavaScript code in mycommandfile.htm. This is typically used for tasks that are too lengthy or complex to be included in the link itself. This file must be an HTML file located in Contribute's Configuration/Command folder

- file (optional*): The file attribute points to an HTML file that provides the user with instructions on how to accomplish the task

- enabled (optional): The default value for enabled is True, which means this task will appear in the *How Do I...* panel. When set to False, the task does not appear

- style (optional): If you want to specify a custom style for the task name as it appears, you can specify it using the style attribute. Note that the attribute value must be the name of a style defined in the tasks.css file. The default style is clsTask

- update (optional): The update attribute provides the same functionality in the <task> element as it does in the <category> element. It checks to see if the task's enabled attribute should be set to True as certain events occur (the same ones as for <category> – see above)

> * Although command, commandfile, *and* file *are all optional attributes, you must specify at least one of these three in each* <task> *element.*

Changing the Layout

The default layout of the *How Do I...* Panel is defined in the TasksLayout.xml file, in the same location as Tasks.xml. It controls the layout, including line height and margins (it is set out in a classic HTML <table> layout). To modify the layout, we modify the table cell (<td>) attributes in the TasksLayout.xml file, found inside the <task_separator> and <category_separator> elements.

Spacing

To increase the vertical space between tasks, modify the `<task_separator>` element. The default for this element is:

```
<task_separator>
  <![CDATA[
  <tr>
    <td colspan="2" height="4"></td>
  </tr>
  ]]>
</task_separator>
```

To reduce the spacing between tags, we decrease the cell `height` value; to increase it, we increase the cell `height`. For example, the following series of screenshots shows the default *How Do I...* panel, followed by a look at the effect caused when we change the `<td>` height attribute (from 4) to 1 and 8 respectively:

Changing the spacing between tasks on the How Do I... panel.

Margins

To adjust the margins of the tasks' container tables, you adjust the `cellspacing` attribute of the `<table>` element inside the `<main>` element. The default settings for this element are:

```
<main>
  <![CDATA[
  <table border="0" cellpadding="0" cellspacing="0" width="100%">
    <tr>
      <td>{category_sections+category_separators}</td>
    </tr>
  </table>
  ]]>
</main>
```

Adding a New Section and Task

The default value for the `cellspacing` attribute is 0; to widen the margins, you can increase it. For example, this screenshot shows the result of changing it to 25:

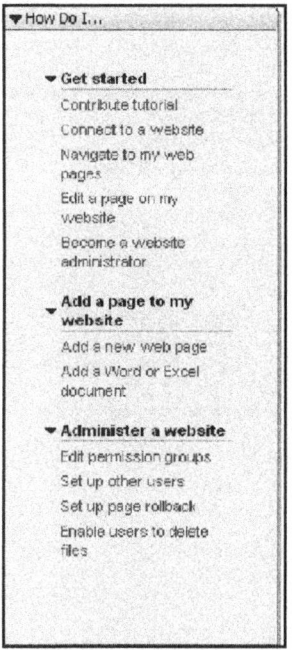

Increasing the table margins of the How Do I... panel.

Now we have seen how to change the layout of our *How Do I...* panel, we will go back to `Tasks.xml`, add a new task, and place it in its own category. We will call our category *Custom Tasks*, and our task *My Task*.

We want our users to find our special task information, so we will make it the first category. Open `Tasks.xml` and add the following code straight after the opening `<tasks>` tag:

```
<category name="Custom Tasks" id="myCategory1">
  <task name="My Task" file="taskMyTask.htm" id="myTask1" />
</category>
```

Now when we launch Contribute, the *How Do I* panel appears like this:

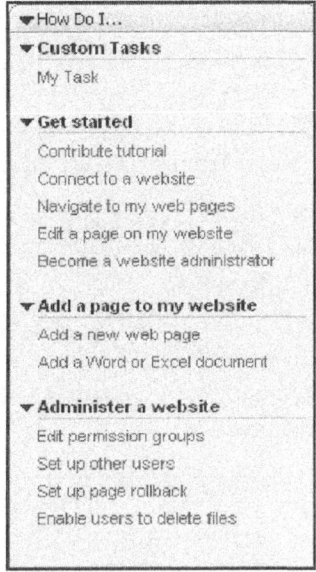

The How Do I... panel, with our new category and task added.

This is all well and good, but it would be nice to actually have an information page sitting there for when the user clicks on the *My Task* link, so let's add one! Now we'll create the task file we referred to in our code (`taskMyTask.htm`) and add it to the `Tasks` folder. Note that it doesn't really matter what you call your task, as long as the name of the HTML files and the `<task> file` attribute value match up.

You might think it complicated to have to build an entire new web page for each topic, but you don't really need to – you can always take one of the existing task pages and modify it and, this way, the *Back* and *Topics* links will already be set up. (Later in this chapter we will go into depth regarding the JavaScript calls for creating links in the *How Do I...* panel.) These pages are contained in the same folder as our XML files.

First, save a copy of one of these task files as `taskMyTask.htm` (we used `task28.htm` – *Add a Word or Excel document*). Now we need to delete everything we don't need, and replace it with our new task information. Delete everything after the first `</table>` tag, and before the closing `<body>` and `</html>` tags.

Now we'll add the instructions on how to perform *My Task* – if we want to keep the layout of our task consistent with the other task pages, we need to add our instructions immediately below the one remaining table (that is, below the `</table>` tag). The code to add is as follows:

```
<table width="100%" border="0" cellpadding="0" cellspacing="0">
  <tr>
    <td class="heading2">
      <p>My Task</p>
      <img height="1" src="images/pixel_white.gif" width="1">
    </td>
  </tr>
```

```
    </table>
    <table width="100%" border="0" cellspacing="0" cellpadding="1">
      <tr>
        <td>
          <p class="customtask">This explains how to do my task:</p>
          <ol>
          <li class="customtask">
            <a href="#"
onMouseUp="dw.tasksPalette.browseToPage('taskMytask1.htm')">Step1</a>
          </li>
          <li class="customtask">Step2</li>
          <li class="customtask">Step3</li>
          </ol>
        </td>
      </tr>
    </table>
```

After we have added our code and saved our HTML page, when we click on the *My Task* link in the *Custom Tags* category, we will now see:

We'll go into more detail about using JavaScript API functions for navigation later in this chapter.

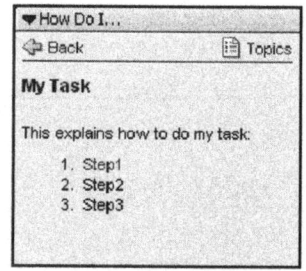

Our custom task page.

You will notice when you try this out that *Step 1* is a different color. This is because we have linked it to another file to explain *Step 1* in more detail. Navigation in the *How Do I...* panel is accomplished using the `onMouseUp` JavaScript event . In this case, we call the JavaScript function `dw.tasksPalette.browseToPage()` event handler. The complete link looks like this:

```
<a href="#" onMouseUp="dw.tasksPalette.browseToPage('taskMytask1.htm')">Step1</a>
```

Now we need to add the target file of the *Step1* link, `taskMytask1.htm`, into our *Tasks* folder (this file can be found in the code download for this chapter, as can a complete version of `taskMyTask.htm`). Now when we click on *Step 1*, the *How Do I...* panel displays the following:

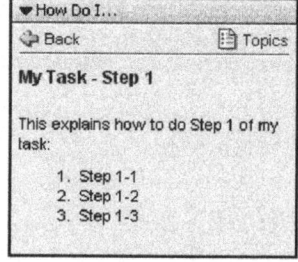

More explanation on Step 1 of our custom task page.

Changing the Default Styles

The `Tasks.css` file (found in the same place as our XML and HTML task files) defines the styles used in the *How Do I...* panel. The default body and table cell styles are as follows:

```css
body {
   font-family: Arial;
   font-size: 11px;
   margin: 2px;
}
td {
   font-family: Arial;
   font-size: 11px;
   padding: 0px;
}
```

Changing the default body style will change the appearance of the text in the *How Do I...* panel. Change the `font-family` to `'Times New Roman'` and increase the `font-size` to `20px` – the code should now look like this:

```css
body {
   font-family: 'Times New Roman';
   font-size: 20px;
   margin: 2px;
}
td {
   font-family: 'Times New Roman';
   font-size: 20px;
   padding: 0px;
}
```

When you have saved your CSS file and restarted Contribute, the *How Do I...* panel will now look something like this:

You could also create new styles, add them to `Tasks.css`, and then apply them to your text. Feel free to experiment with the look of your pages using CSS. Now let's go on to something more challenging...

The How Do I... panel, after our font change.

Navigating Between Task Documents Using JavaScript

Links in task documents are always created using the `onMouseUp` JavaScript event handler. As we saw earlier, the syntax is:

```
<a href="#" onMouseUp="dw.tasksPalette.functionname()">Link Text</a>
```

or, if an argument is required to provide the value for a JavaScript variable (such as a document name):

```
<a href="#" onMouseUp="dw.tasksPalette.functionname('argument1') ">Link Text</a>
```

Three API functions offered in Contribute are as follows:

- `dw.tasksPalette.back()`: This function will take the user back to the previously viewed page in the *How Do I...* panel. If there is no previous page in the panel history, it will take the user to the main *How Do I...* panel, which is Topics. Its syntax is simply `dw.tasksPalette.back()`.

- `dw.tasksPalette.browseToPage()`: The `dw.tasksPalette. browseToPage(strRelativePath)` function displays the page specified in the argument. If no argument is specified, the user is returned to the main *How Do I* panel. It has one argument, `strRelativePath`, which is the relative pathname of the file the user will be taken to after clicking on the link. Example syntax is as follows:

```
<a href="#" onMouseUp="dw.tasksPalette.browseToPage
          ('taskMytask.htm')">
   Task Name
</a>
```

- `dw.tasksPalette.expandSection(strItemIdentification)`: This function is only used in `TasksLayout.xml`. It expands or collapses a category in the *How Do I...* section when a category name is clicked. It has two arguments, `bExpand`, which is set to `True` if the category should be expanded and `False` if it should be collapsed, and `strItemIdentification`, which is the value of the `category.id` that needs to be expanded or collapsed (if this argument is empty, nothing will happen when the user clicks on the category). Example syntax is as follows:

```
dw.tasksPalette.expandSection(true, "8")
```

Using Images in the How Do I Panel

You can use any images you want to use in the *How Do I...* panel by putting them in the `Tasks/images` folder, then referencing them as you would any other image in an HTML document, for example:

```
<img src="images/taskback.gif" alt="Back" border="0" align="absmiddle">
```

Macromedia supplies the following images:

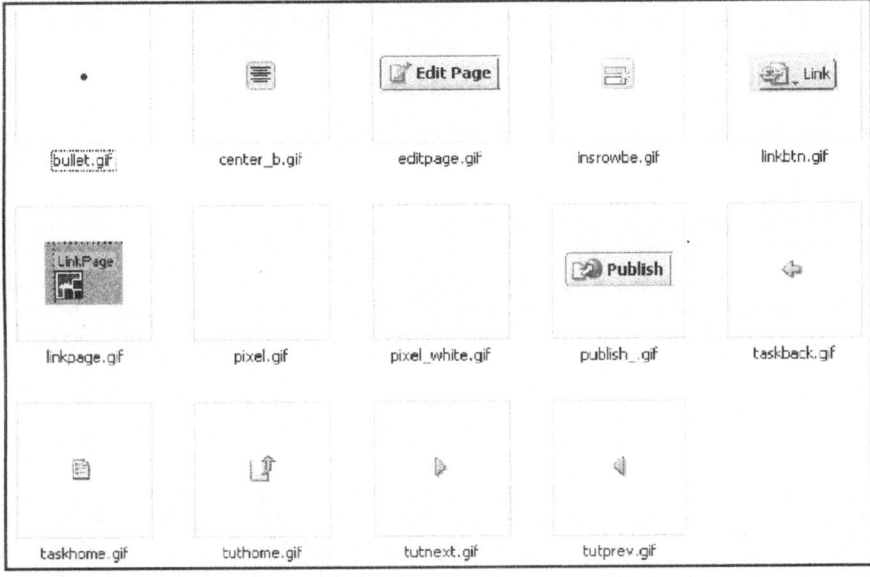

Contribute Preferences

Contribute offers the user several setup preferences . It's a good idea to understand these so that you can recommend the optimum settings to your user, and provide an initial configuration that will work for each user.

To configure preferences, select *Edit > Preferences*. There are four sections – *General*, *File Editors*, *Firewall*, and *Invisible Elements*.

General Preferences

General Preferences has three settings, *Faster table editing*, *Spelling dictionary*, and *Microsoft Word and Excel documents*:

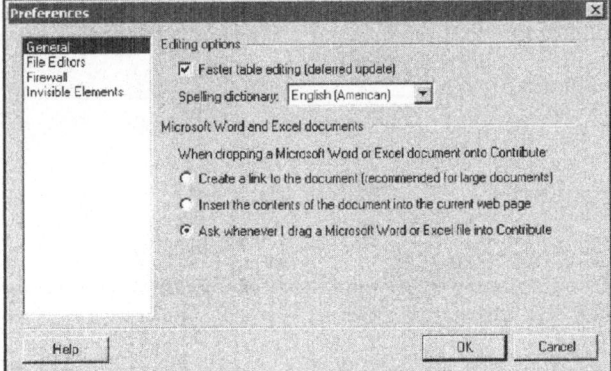

Contribute General Preferences.

Faster table editing is much the same as the corresponding option in Dreamweaver. By checking this box, you make sure that tables will not be redrawn while you are editing table content, thereby speeding up the process. When you click outside the table, it will be redrawn to reflect any changes that were generated by editing the table's content. This box is checked by default.

Spelling dictionary provides a dropdown list of languages to use for spell checking. It lists all of the languages available to Contribute and provides distinct dictionaries for American English and British English.

Microsoft Word and Excel documents allows you to choose how text is treated when you drag content from Microsoft Word and Excel. You can choose to create a link to the originating document, insert the contents directly into the current page, or have Contribute prompt you to decide between these two options each time you drag content from Word or Excel. Creating a link is recommended for large documents. I prefer to decide each time I drag content in since the content dragged in can vary in size.

File Editors

In this screen, you can select the applications used to edit various file types. You can add and remove extensions and configure more than one editor for any given file type, such as images, text files, and Microsoft Office documents. If more than one editor is provided, you can designate one of them as the primary editor for that file type. If only one editor is listed, that application is automatically designated as the primary or default editor. Items are added and removed from each list using the + and − buttons.

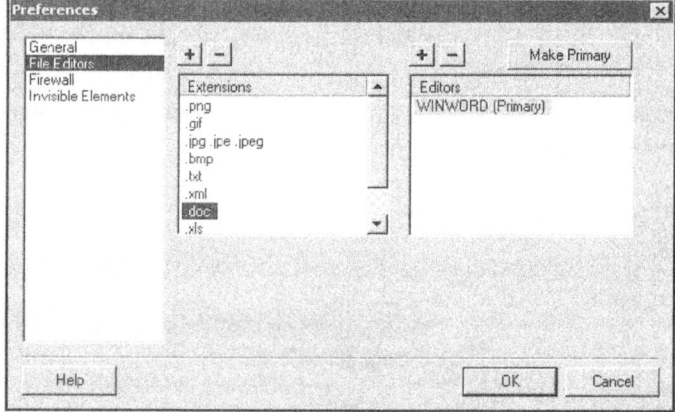

File Editor Preferences

Firewall

If your users are working from behind a firewall, you will need to provide Contribute with the hostname and port for the firewall in order to make a connection to the remote site. The *Firewall* screen is where this is done.

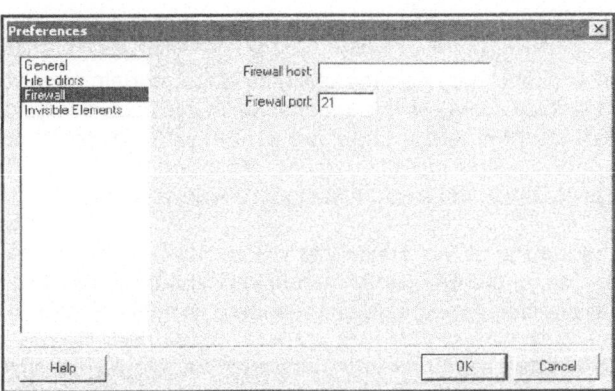

Firewall Preferences

Invisible Elements

Check the option labeled *Show section anchors when editing a page* if your users will need to edit named anchors on pages to create links within pages. The anchors will appear only in Edit mode. This will allow users to select the name anchors and edit their properties, even though these anchors do not appear in the browser.

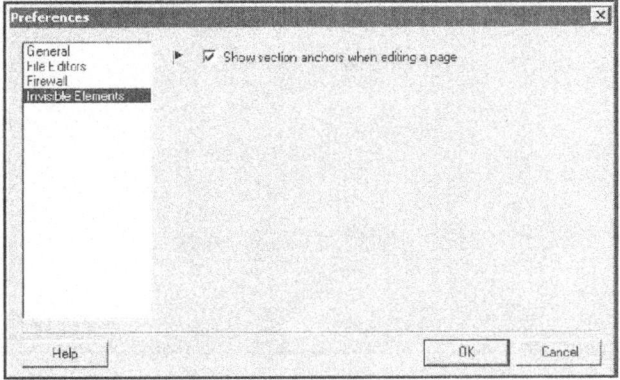

Invisible Elements Preferences.

Customizing User Groups

In this section we're going to discuss some of your options for controlling the workflow, and what your users can and can't do. *Chapter 5* will discuss setting permissions for design activities, and also offers some best practices. You can also:

- Control the folders users can update
- Grant or deny permission to create and delete pages
- Configure default settings for blank pages
- Use inherited Dreamweaver MX Extensibility

Setting Up Multiple User Groups and Permissions

You may have some users that need the ability to edit a certain folder or create new pages, and others who shouldn't have access to this folder at all. In this case it's useful to set up multiple groups for users. Let's start with the default *Users* group in the *Administer Website* dialog box, which you get by going to *Edit > Administer Websites*, choosing your site, then entering the correct administration password (we first saw these screens in *Chapter 2*).

You should now be looking at the *Administer Website* Dialog box. From here, highlight the *Users* permission group, click on the *Edit Group* button, and click on *Folder/File Access* from the left-hand menu in the next dialog that appears, to be presented with this screen:

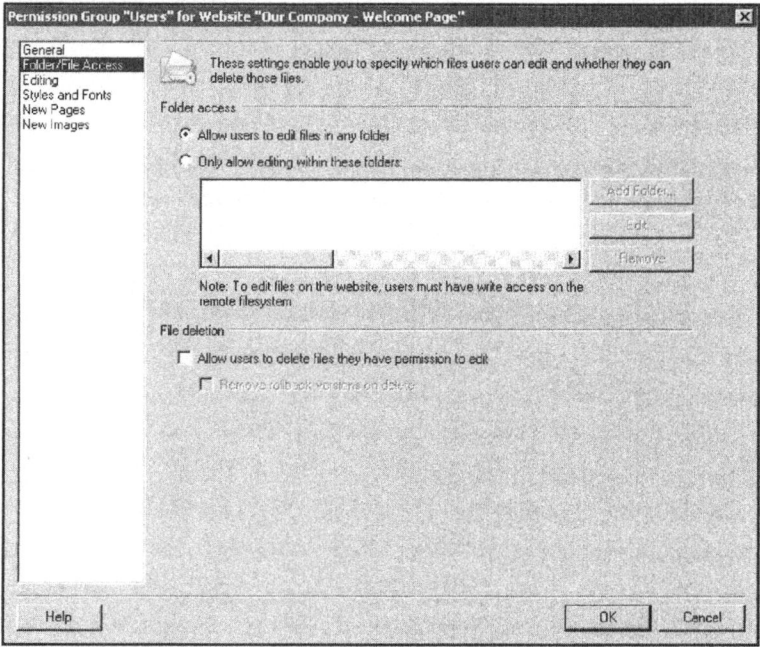

Setting user permissions.

In this screen, the default setting allows all users to edit all folders. This is fine for advanced users/administrators, but in most cases we will only want contributors to have access to the files they need to edit.

For example, in our sample site, say the only folder we want to give contributors access to is the `about` folder. Click the radiobutton *Only allow editing within these folders*, and then the newly-enabled *Add Folder* button. This will bring up a *Choose Folder* dialog box for us to choose the folder we want to give access to. Double-click on the `about` folder, then click the button that is now labeled *Select 'about'*. You will now be returned to the previous dialog box, which will now look like this:

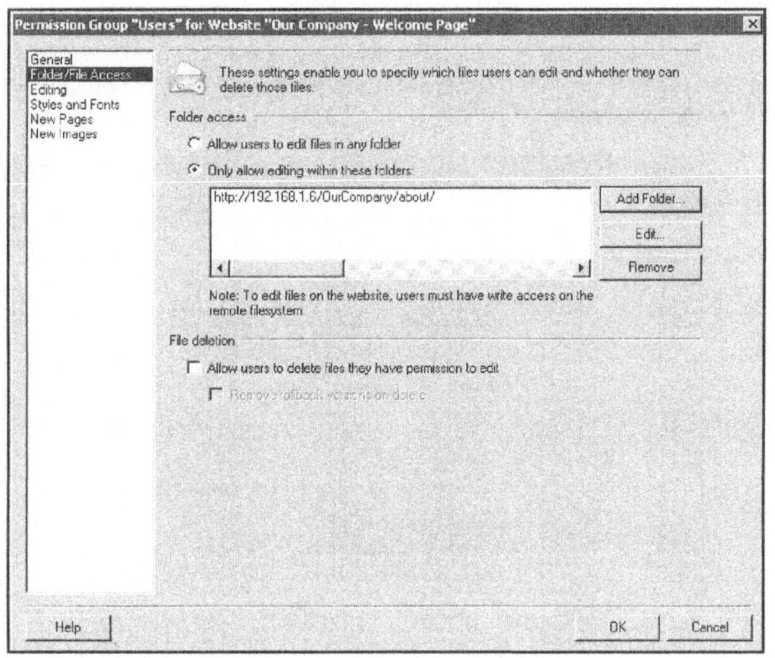

Our users can now only edit pages within the about folder.

Our contributors can now only modify pages inside the about folder. In addition, we will keep the *Allow users to delete files they have permission to edit* checkbox unchecked, so they can't go deleting files.

Now we'll prevent the general *Users* group from creating new pages. In the same dialog box, click on the *New Pages* option in the left-hand menu. In this dialog box, simply uncheck all the checkboxes, then click *OK* to return to the *Administer Website* dialog.

Note: You cannot prevent users from editing specific files or subfolders in folders that they have access to. However, in Dreamweaver MX, you can permanently Check Out any files you wish to protect from being edited.

Creating an Advanced User Group

Next, we'll create a group called *Advanced Users*. We want these users to retain the same permission settings for editing and styles as our standard users, so we'll copy the existing *Users* group. In the *Administer Website* dialog, select *Users*, then click the *Duplicate* button; type in the name *Advanced Users* to the *Permission Group Name* dialog that appears, and then click *OK*.

Now highlight our new user group and click the *Edit Group...* button to be returned to the *Permission Group* dialog we've seen above. We'll give this group permission to edit files in all folders – click on the *Folder/File Access* option in the left-hand menu, then click on the *Allow users to edit files in any folder* radio button.

We'll also allow users in this group to add new pages by using existing pages and templates only. We can select which templates, if any are available to users for creating new pages (see *Chapter 7* for more on using templates with Contribute). Click on the *New Pages* option in the left-hand menu to bring up the following screen:

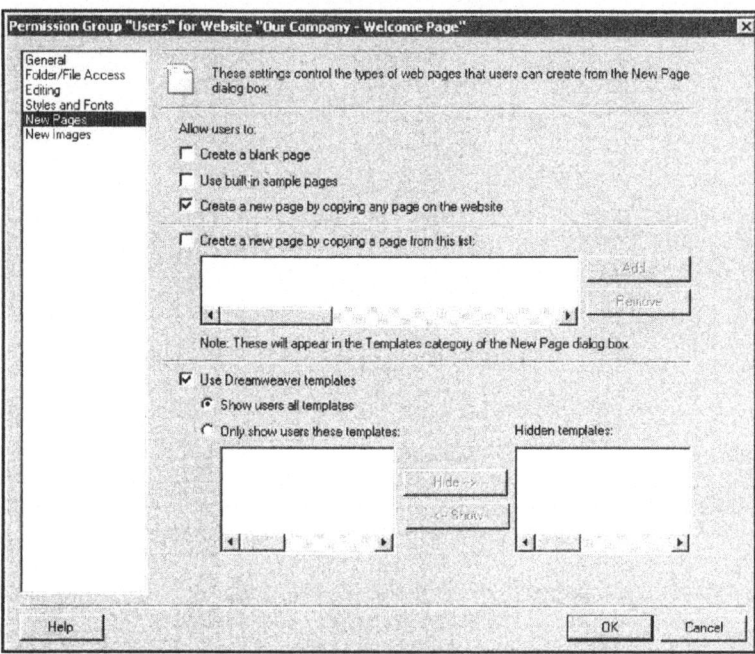

Setting the options your users have available when creating new pages.

Check the two checkboxes labeled *Create a new page by copying any page on the website*, and *Use Dreamweaver templates*. If you have any templates available, you can make them available here (in the code download for this chapter, you can find a template called `newpage.dwt` that you could use).

If a page you specified for basing new pages upon is deleted from the server, make sure to remove it from the New Pages selection for each user group. Otherwise, the users will see the 404 error page when they browse to the page in the new page dialog box, and they will receive an error message if they try to create a new page based on the missing page.

Using a Custom Default New Page

Finally, rather than allowing the users to create new pages based on any page on the site, we could also select a specific page (or specific pages) they can use to create new pages from. This can be any page located on the server, including a Dreamweaver template. (Dreamweaver templates provide the advantage of more control over the elements of a page that the user can edit, as opposed to traditional HTML pages.) We then add the pages we want them to be able to use. These pages will then appear in the templates available when the user goes to create a new page (*File > New Page...*).

It is a good idea to give users a single template (or a couple if needed) to create new pages from, from the point of view of site consistency. You can choose to use an existing Dreamweaver template, or an HTML page.

Whichever page you choose to use for this purpose, when it is ready, upload it to a suitable folder on your server. Now go back to the *New Pages* options, uncheck the two options we previously checked, and as mentioned above, check the *Create a new page by copying a page from this list* option. Now you need to add your template into the box below by clicking the *Add...* button and navigating to your template.

Customizing the Default File Extension

The default file extension for new pages in Contribute is `.htm`. But suppose you want your users creating pages that end in `.html` or `.asp`? All you need to do is follow the same procedure outlined above, but ensure that all of the pages you make available have the file extension you want your users to use. This will work with all pages EXCEPT template-based pages.

Enabling Contribute to Work with Screen Readers

By default, Contribute does not work with screen readers, such as JAWS and Window-Eyes. Enabling this function creates issues with Contribute's text-editing capabilities, and even with it enabled, screen readers cannot read all of the dialog boxes.

If you have users that need to use a screen reader, you will need to modify `ScreenreaderSupport.htm`, which you should be able to find in `Configuration\Startup\`.

In this file, you need to change line 15 from

```
Var USING_SCREENREADER = false;
```

to

```
Var USING_SCREENREADER = true;
```

Save the file and, when you restart Contribute, the screen reader will be enabled. Since this is applied on the user's PC, it will only affect the individual Contribute user who needs to make use of the screen reader.

Inherited Dreamweaver MX Extensibility

Contribute inherits a good deal of extensibility from Dreamweaver MX. If you are not familiar with Dreamweaver MX's extensibility features, or do not have access to Dreamweaver MX, refer to the online documentation at *http://www.macromedia.com/support/dreamweaver/extend.html*.

We won't go into great detail about each feature. If you're familiar with Dreamweaver MX extensibility, these are mostly self-explanatory. These are the Dreamweaver-inherited extensibility features available in Contribute:

- **Menus**: You can customize menus by adding or removing functions using Contribute's API functions, and launch new extensions such as objects, commands, and floating panels. For instance, you may want to add topics to the *Help* menu. Menus are defined in `%Contribute%\Configuration\Menus\ccmenus.xml`

- **Toolbars**: You can create and modify toolbars in Contribute. They function similarly to menus, but provide visual icons for triggering events. Custom toolbar files can be added to the user configuration files in `Configuration\Toolbars`

- **Objects**: You can add new objects to Contribute. By default they will appear in the **Insert** menu and can use a modal user interface. They can insert predefined blocks of code or text within the current document. Objects are useful for commonly used HTML snippets such as links, headers, and footers

- **Commands**: Commands appear at the bottom of the Format menu by default. They are similar to objects but more powerful because they can modify the page using the JavaScript 1.4 Document Object Model. Commands are modal. For more information on the Document Object Model, you can visit *http://www.mozilla.org/docs/dom/*

- **Floating Panels**: Floating panels are modeless. They can accept user input to modify the page and display information about the page

- **Translators**: Translators are used to control the editing experience. They are used to provide a design-time representation of code elements and tags

- **Third Party Tags**: You can define your own tags to identify blocks of content. Other extensions often make use of them in order to perform operations

- **JavaScript Extensions**: Extensions can provide new APIs that you can call from JavaScript. They can be written in any language and must be compiled as a Dynamic Link Library (DLL)

Summary

In this chapter, we discussed some different ways in which you can customize Contribute to better meet your own needs, and those of your users. Specifically, we looked at:

- Modifying the Contribute Welcome page
- Modifying the *How Do I...* section
- Contribute Preferences
- Customizing User Groups
- Customizing the new pages your users can choose from
- Enabling Contribute to work with screen readers
- Inherited Dreamweaver MX extensibility

Customizing Contribute

In this Chapter

- Protecting coding standards

- Setting style permissions

- Setting permissions for new images and pages

- Accessibility options

Author: Brandon Heffernan

Best Practices

To get the most out of Contribute there are several techniques and principles you can apply to a web site from the outset. Effective coding practices can help create a simplified and understandable environment in which your Contribute users can work. It can also help you to ensure the integrity of the code and style conventions you establish.

In this chapter, we'll explore how to set up your web site for optimal use within Contribute, and how to use Contribute's administrative settings to enforce your style guide, prevent users from adding unwanted code, and ensure that the web site is optimized for accessibility.

Enforcing Code and Style Conventions

If you author your web site according to code and style parameters that you established during your planning phase, you'll likely want to guarantee that your Contribute users adhere to those standards when your web site is live. Contribute makes it easy for you to "lock in" your site-wide styles, to preserve the overall look and feel of your site and make it easy for users to choose from the styles you make available.

Protect Your Code Standards

If the integrity of your HTML or XHTML code is important to you, make sure you include a DOCTYPE tag on each page of your site that declares your intended document type and version. For example, if you decide to author your site with XHTML, you'll want to make sure that any changes made by Contribute users will be made with XHTML code.

To achieve this, you first need to develop your web site so that Contribute can follow your coding guidelines. Then, make sure you include the appropriate DOCTYPE tag at the top of all pages in your site.

The most common document types are the strict and transitional versions of either HTML 4.01 or XHTML 1.0:

```
<!DOCTYPE html PUBLIC "-//W3C//DTD XHTML 1.0 Strict//EN"
"http://www.w3.org/TR/xhtml1/DTD/xhtml1-strict.dtd">

<!DOCTYPE html PUBLIC "-//W3C//DTD XHTML 1.0 Transitional//EN"
"http://www.w3.org/TR/xhtml1/DTD/xhtml1-transitional.dtd">

<!DOCTYPE HTML PUBLIC "-//W3C//DTD HTML 4.01//EN"
   "http://www.w3.org/TR/html4/strict.dtd">

<!DOCTYPE HTML PUBLIC "-//W3C//DTD HTML 4.01 Transitional//EN">
```

Contribute will adhere to whichever coding standard you choose. Contribute uses the Dreamweaver MX authoring engine, which automatically generates standards-compliant code based on the document type declaration (DTD) you declare on each page. Contribute also prevents users from accidentally or deliberately adding non-compliant HTML code to your web pages (ensure `<br />` tags are used in XHTML documents, for example).

You don't have to manually type or even copy and paste your desired DOCTYPE tag into every page of your site. Dreamweaver MX allows you to select the DOCTYPE you want your page code to adhere to, and it then automatically inserts the correct tag into every new page you create. Once you have done this, you don't have to do anything else in Contribute – the changes that users make in Contribute will be made with the coding standards you establish.

Setting Style Permissions

Contribute makes it easy for you to enforce your style conventions across all the pages in your web site. When users edit a page, they are presented with menus and buttons, which they can use to change text styles. By default, Contribute provides users with menu and button options that resemble most word processing programs. For example, Contribute provides buttons for bold and italic styles, text alignment options, text color, background color, list, and indent options.

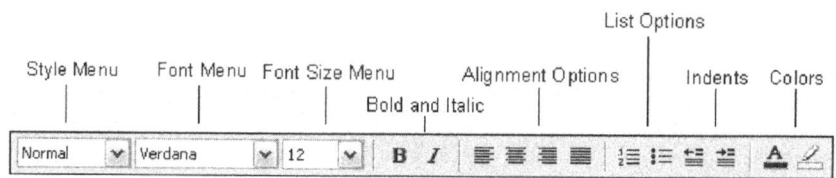

The Contribute styling toolbar.

You can also control whether or not some of these tools are available to users. You can set permissions for users or specific groups among your users, which will prevent them from making unwanted content or style changes. For example, if you prevent users from changing font faces and font sizes, then the *Font Menu* and *Font Size Menu* will not be available when users open your web site pages in Contribute. You control these and other style permissions from the *Permission Group* dialog box.

Managing Permission Groups

To set style permissions, Choose *Edit > Administer Websites*, and select your web site. When you log in with your administrator password, the *Administer Website* dialog box appears. Make sure that *Users* is selected, and then click the *Edit Group* button.

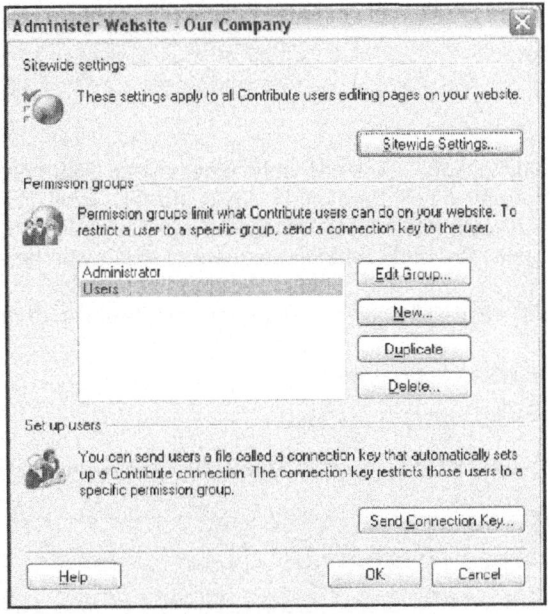

The Administer Website dialog box.

When you click *Edit Group*, the *Permission Groups* dialog box appears. Click on the *Styles and Fonts* category to display the administrative options for styles and fonts. From this dialog box, you can control your users' editorial privileges.

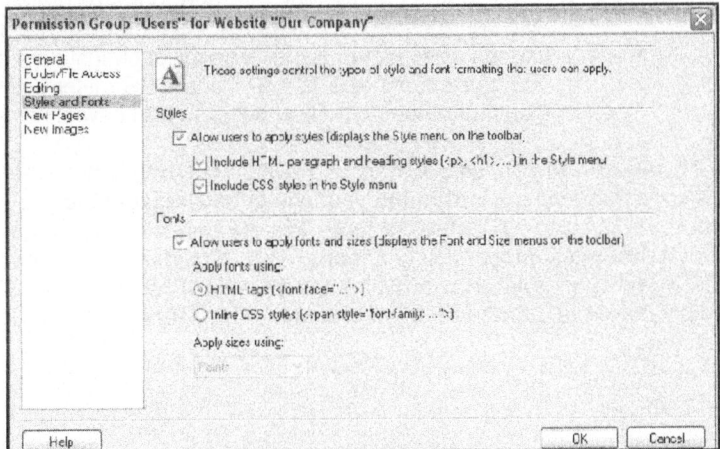

The Permission Group dialog box.

The first option in this dialog box *Allow users to apply styles*, will enable or disable the *Style* menu. The *Style* menu allows users to apply standard HTML tag-based styles, or your custom CSS styles.

If you uncheck the *Include HTML paragraph and heading styles* option, users won't be able to apply general HTML tag-based styles (`<p>`, `<h1>`, and so forth). This can help to preserve the integrity of your code and prevent users from adding new tags to your HTML. If you leave this option checked, Contribute inserts HTML heading tags when a user selects them from the *Style* menu. Allowing Contribute users to introduce new HTML can harm your document structure. Your goal should be to preserve the integrity of your code while allowing users to apply styles that are customized for general use.

When this option is unchecked, users can only access your CSS classes to apply styles. When a user chooses a custom class from the *Style* menu, Contribute writes the appropriate `class="classname"` attribute into the tag that the selected text is defined by. This is a better method because it prevents unwanted code and forces users to work with the styles you have created.

For best quality control while still allowing your users the flexibility to make style changes:

- Check *Allow users to apply styles*

- Check *Include CSS styles in the Style* menu

- Uncheck *Include HTML paragraph and heading styles*, as shown below:

Allowing users to style content via CSS, but not via HTML paragraphs and headings gives good results.

In Contribute, indented options like these indicate that their "parent" option must be selected before you can activate them.

In the *Fonts* section of this dialog box, you can determine whether users will have access to font faces and font sizes. Enabling this option allows users to change the font face and font size of text on a page. You can also control *how* Contribute applies their font style changes. You can set Contribute to write `<font>` tags for each instance of a style change, or you can enforce the use of inline CSS styles (using the `<span>` tag). Contribute does not allow users to add new styles to a stylesheet.

Remember, the `<font>` tag is deprecated in HTML 4; it has been phased out in favor of stylesheets. If code integrity is important to you, you should disable the `<font>` tag option, since even if the DOCTYPE is set to XHTML Contribute can still insert `<font>` tags if they are enabled. Using CSS styles creates more sizing options, and provides for greater accessibility. We'll explore accessibility options later in this chapter. When you select *Inline CSS Styles*, a drop-down menu activates. This allows you to set the unit of measurement that Contribute will use for all font size changes.

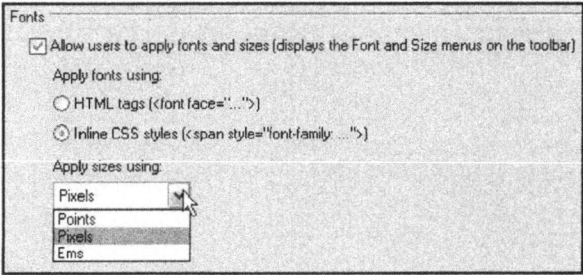

Controlling the user's ability to apply fonts and sizes. It's a good idea to stop users from using deprecated <font> elements.

You can choose from three units of measurement: *Points*, *Pixels*, and *Ems*. Points are a unit of print measurement, and do not translate as well to the screen. You're better off choosing either pixels or ems.

Pixels are a screen unit of measurement, and they result in greater consistency across different browsers and platforms than points. When you set pixels as the default unit of measurement, users will see a menu with the following options:

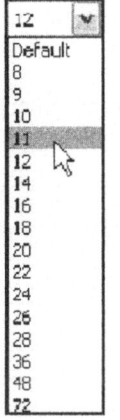

Setting font size in pixels.

Since many web browsers do not allow text defined in pixel sizes to be resized, use of pixel-based sizes can cause accessibility problems for the visually impaired; if accessibility is an issue you may wish to avoid this option. Some modern browsers do allow users to adjust the size of text, even if it's expressed in pixel values, but it's still best to avoid it if possible.

Ems are a *relative* unit of measurement, which means they're set relative to a default or inherited font size. For example, if your default body text is set at 14 pixels, then text set at 2 ems will be equal to 28 pixels. If the default body text is then changed to 12 pixels, the text set at 2 ems will automatically change relative to that size, which would be equivalent to being set at 24 pixels. When you set ems as the default unit of measurement, users will see options expressed in percentage values in the *Font Size Menu*, as shown overleaf.

As a relative unit of measurement, text based on em units will be relative to their parent's font size, which is often the font size set on the body element or the browser's default font size if no size is set for the body element. If a user changes the default text size in his or her browser, all the relative sizes of your text will change accordingly.

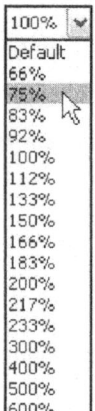

Setting font size in ems.

Contribute displays percentage values so users will intuitively know how much smaller or larger each increment will be. Despite the appearance, **Contribute does not write percentage values into the code**. It uses ems, and calculates the value in ems based on the percentage value that the user selects. (After all, most users won't know what ems are, so displaying a long list of values wouldn't make for a particularly intuitive interface.)

Another option you should consider is to completely disable the font-sizing options. When you uncheck this feature, the options below it appear dimmed out:

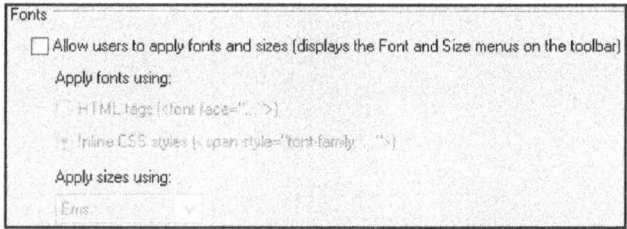

You might even want to stop users from changing fonts and font sizes altogether.

When you disable the font settings feature, the Contribute interface will not show the *Font* menu or *Font Size* menu. Depending on the nature of your web site, your users, and groups, this can have distinct advantages. New users might be eager to make font changes based on personal preference, and personal preference is rarely a priority in matters of web design. If all your users change font faces on various pages according to their preferences, you can throw your intended design and style conventions out the window.

If you decide to disable the font settings feature, your users will still be able to change text styles using the *Style* menu, which contains a list of any CSS classes you have in your stylesheet. As we discussed earlier, it's arguably best to limit users' style options to the CSS styles you create in your stylesheets. To optimize the effectiveness of the *Style* menu, you'll need to follow a few simple guidelines when you first create your web site, which follow below.

Create Logically-Named Style Classes

If you decide to allow your users to make style changes to text, you can use these style classes to create a palette of pre-set styles that they can choose from using the *Style Menu*. This allows users to contribute to the look and feel of your web pages without fear of breaking any style conventions.

When you develop your web site's CSS styles, it's critical that you create class names that will make sense to your Contribute users. Your class names will appear in the *Style* menu, and if they're not named logically, your users won't know what they're meant for. For example, if you create different styles for heading types, use logically named classes, such as:

```
.mainHeading { main heading styles here }
.subHeading  { sub heading styles here }
.footer      { footer text styles here }
```

This allows users to easily determine what each style is meant to perform. When the *Style* menu is activated, your class styles appear as options in the drop-down menu, making it easy for users to apply your styles, as shown below:

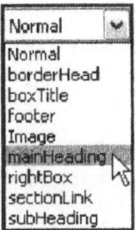

Having logically-named CSS styles is an advantage.

If your document contains a top-level heading that's defined with an `<h1>` tag, a Contribute user can select this text and style it with any of the classes in the drop-down menu. For example, if a user selects the `mainHeading` style, Contribute will write the following code into the HTML:

```
<h1 class="mainHeading">
```

However, Contribute will allow the user to apply the `mainHeading` style to any piece of text, even one which is not a heading (using the code `<span class="mainHeading"></span>`). A solution for this problem would be to create a CSS style of the form:

```
h1.mainHeading { main heading styles here }
```

so that the `mainHeading` style is limited to `<h1>` tags. However, Contribute will still only show the class name in the *Style* menu – not the fact that it is related to the `<h1>` tag. This could cause confusion for users if they attempt to add the style to a non-`<h1>` piece of text and nothing happens. Care should be taken with these options, and advice on use of styles provided to users, so that problems can be avoided.

Hide Classes from the Style Menu

Contribute's *Style* menu normally displays every class you have in your stylesheet. Some of your class styles might not be appropriate for random use by your contributors. If you don't want a particular class style to display in the *Style* menu, you can rename the class in your stylesheet so that it begins with `.mmhide_`. For example, if you have the following class style:

```
.linkBox { background-color: #abc; }
```

You can prevent this class from showing up in the *Style* menu by changing the name to:

```
.mmhide_linkBox { background-color: #abc; }
```

You don't have to change any HTML - your classes will still work normally. You will likely find that this technique is extremely valuable, especially if you manage a large web site that contains several classes not intended for general use.

Show/Hide HTML Styles in the Style Menu

As mentioned earlier, you can uncheck the *Include HTML paragraph and heading styles* option so that users won't be able to insert new heading tags. By default, Contribute includes default heading tags as style options in the *Style* menu, along with your classes. If you don't disable this option, users will see something like this:

The Style menu will look like this if you allow users to use HTML headings and paragraphs.

These generic heading styles can be confusing to users, and can create unwanted results. For example, if users see custom styles *and* generic heading styles, they might not know which heading styles to apply. It may also result in arbitrary use of styles by different users.

As mentioned before, Contribute inserts new heading tags wherever a user applies these styles. If you don't want your users introducing new heading structures into your pages, you should disable this feature. Establishing the structure of your web pages is best left in *your* domain, and coded into the templates you create; it shouldn't be left in the hands of less experienced users. When you set your style and font privileges, take these factors into consideration. The guidelines mentioned in this chapter will help you to both protect and reinforce the look and feel of your site.

Editing Preferences

The *Permission Group* dialog box also allows you to control editing behaviors for your users. From the *Permission Group* dialog box, click on the *Editing* category to display your options.

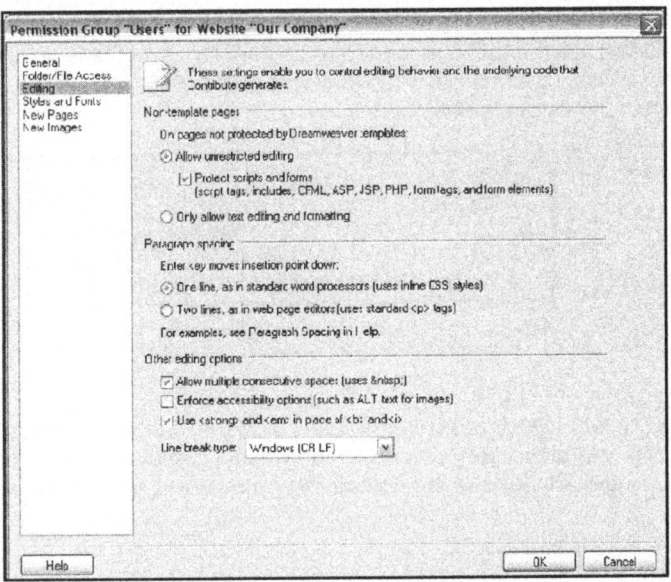

Further controlling users' editing capabilities using the Editing category of the Permission Group dialog box.

This dialog box provides additional methods for controlling the code that Contribute generates. The first section of this dialog box, *Non-template pages*, enables you to control the kind of code your users will have access to. Contribute is optimized to work with Dreamweaver MX, but you can use Contribute to manage any web site, no matter what program was used to create it.

Managing Sites Not Built with Dreamweaver MX Templates

The primary advantage to using Contribute with web sites built with Dreamweaver MX is the powerful template features that Dreamweaver provides. Dreamweaver templates prevent users from accessing 'fixed' areas of a page – areas that you don't want anyone to edit or modify in any way.

If you use Contribute to manage a web site that was not built with Dreamweaver MX, you'll need to make sure that any critical code within your web pages (either client-side or server-side code) cannot be modified or deleted by any code changes that Contribute users make. To do this, make sure that the *Protect scripts and forms* option is checked, as shown below:

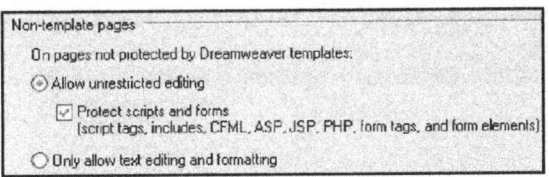

You shouldn't allow all your users to have access to the code on your pages: make sure this option stays checked, unless you have a specific permission group that needs access to the code.

This option is checked by default, for good reason. If some Contribute users require access to scripts and forms, make sure you set up a specific user group with these access privileges for qualified users: don't extend them to your entire Contribute team.

More often than not, you won't want your Contribute users making preferential changes to your page layouts and vital content areas. If you need to limit the permissions of your Contribute users to simple functions, like adding text content and modifying content styles, you should also check the *Only allow text editing and formatting* option. If you do select this option, Contribute displays a message to users, as shown in the screenshot below:

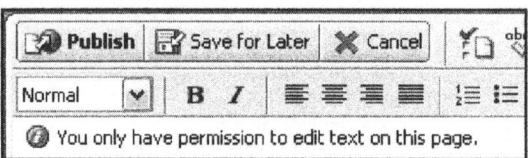

This is message is displayed when users try to do things they cannot when you have only given them editing and formatting priviledges.

With this setting, users will not be able to insert or delete tables, images, or links. Keep in mind, however, that this will only apply to non-Dreamweaver templates. If you're using Dreamweaver templates, this feature will not override the editing permissions you set up in your templates.

Paragraph-Spacing Options

You can control how Contribute creates paragraphs when users press the *Enter* key. In most word processing programs, pressing the *Enter* key moves the insertion point down one line, like a typewriter's 'carriage return'. You can set Contribute to follow this paragraph spacing, or you can set it to create a new paragraph every time users press the *Enter* key.

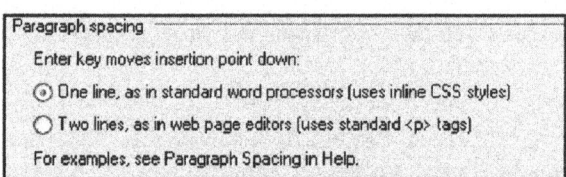

Setting Contribute to either use CSS styles or simple HTML <p> elements when the Enter key is pressed.

When the first option, *One line*, is selected, Contribute writes inline CSS styles into each paragraph tag. The styles remove the default top and bottom margins that a paragraph tag creates. For example, if you write a paragraph of text and press *Enter*, Contribute writes the following code:

```
<p style="margin-top: 0; margin-bottom: 0;">Your New Line of Text</p>
```

In *One line* mode, pressing the *Enter* key twice removes the inline style in favor of a standard paragraph tag.

The second option, *Two lines*, creates simple paragraph tags without any inline styles, every time a user presses the *Enter* key. The insertion point moves down two lines each time the *Enter* key is pressed. Contribute writes the following code:

```
<p>Your New Line of Text</p>
```

The image below shows how each of these options will look in a browser:

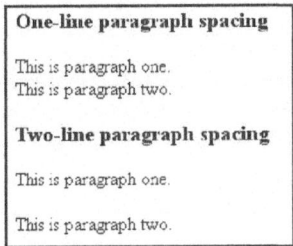

This is how paragraphs will look with the two different available paragraph spacing options.

As always, the settings you choose should partly depend on the experience and comfort level of your Contribute users. In the case of paragraph spacing, you might want to stick with what's most familiar to them. If you use the *One line* option, you can always explain to your users that pressing *Enter* twice will create standard paragraph spacing.

There are drawbacks to the *One line* option. The inline styles that Contribute writes into each paragraph tag to achieve single spacing can add up to a lot of extra code – style information that is not separated from your document structure, which is one of the primary benefits of stylesheets.

Word Spacing Options

The third section of the *Editing* category in the *Permission Groups* dialog box allows you to enable or disable multiple consecutive spaces. Checking this option allows users to create spaces between words by pressing the space bar multiple times. This editing behavior is common in word processing programs, but it can create problems in web pages.

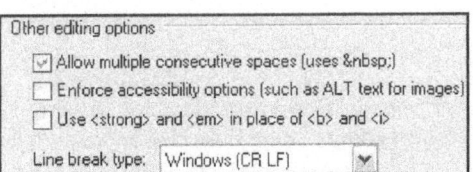

The last options on the Editing category of the Permission Group dialog box. Here we can allow or disallow multiple spaces.

Contribute writes multiple non-breaking space characters ( ) to separate words. Browsers can treat these consecutive spaces differently – some browsers collapse them, honoring only one space at a time. A more serious concern is that some users might attempt to use multiple spaces to achieve a desired layout, which can create a mountain of unnecessary code and a lack of consistent appearance across different browsers.

Arguably, it's a good idea to disable this option. Users won't be able to move the insertion point more than one space at a time, which can help you to ensure proper editing practices, and reinforce the use of your pre-set styles to modify page design.

Enforce Accessibility Options

When you select this option, Contribute will prompt users for accessibility information when inserting images and tables.

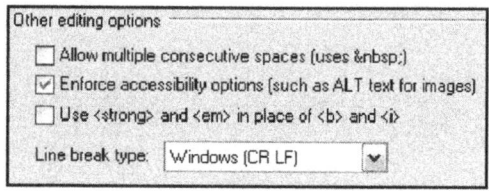

We can also enforce accessibility techniques.

For example, when a user inserts an image, Contribute will prompt the user to enter alternative text for the image. This text will display on the page if the user cannot view images.

This feature is important to any web site project. Several accessibility initiatives, including Section 508 of the Federal Rehabilitation Act (US) and the Office of the e-Envoy (UK), call for web sites to follow specific coding guidelines. Following these guidelines will help make your web content accessible for those users with disabilities who employ screenreaders to scan web content. In some cases you will be legally required to follow these guidelines, so it is important that you set up Contribute to do so.

As a web site administrator, you should be familiar with these guidelines, and how accessibility issues impact your target audience. You can find more information at the following web sites:

- *http://www.w3.org/WAI/*
- *http://www.section508.gov/*

as well as in the book *Accessible Web Sites* (Thatcher et al, glasshaus, ISBN 1-904151-00-0).

Accessible Images

When *Enforce accessibility options* is checked, users will be prompted with the dialog box shown below whenever they insert an image. Contribute prevents users from bypassing this dialog box.

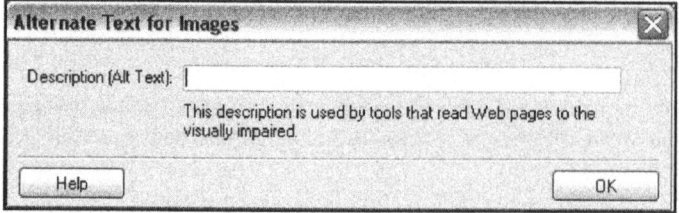

When the Enforce accessibility options option is checked, users will be prompted to enter alt text for all images.

As stated in the dialog box, this alternative text will be read aloud by screenreader software. Also, some users prefer to browse the Web with images disabled, for faster page loading. The content that users enter here will display as an alternative text description for that image. In some browsers, alternative text will also display when the mouse pointer is placed over the image – in the form of a "tooltip".

You should consider providing your Contribute users with a quick reference on how to write effective alternative text. Different situations call for different descriptions. Some situations call for **descriptive text**, and others call for **replacement text**.

For example, if the image is a photograph of a scene of some kind, the alternative text should probably be a brief statement that describes the scene, to ensure that all users will understand what the content depicts. Replacement text is useful when the images themselves contain text. For example, if an image contains the text "*Holiday Specials*", the text alternative for the image should simply duplicate the text in the image. Advice on when to use which form of text should be present in the *Style Guide*, which we will discuss later.

Accessible Tables

You can also guarantee that any tables your users insert will follow basic accessibility guidelines. When you select *Enforce accessibility options*, Contribute inserts the scope attribute into every instance of a table header cell (<th> tag). The value of the scope attribute will either be row or col, which helps screenreaders identify the relationships between table data cells and their corresponding headings, and read them accordingly.

For example, if a user inserts a table, the *Insert Table* dialog box appears, as shown below:

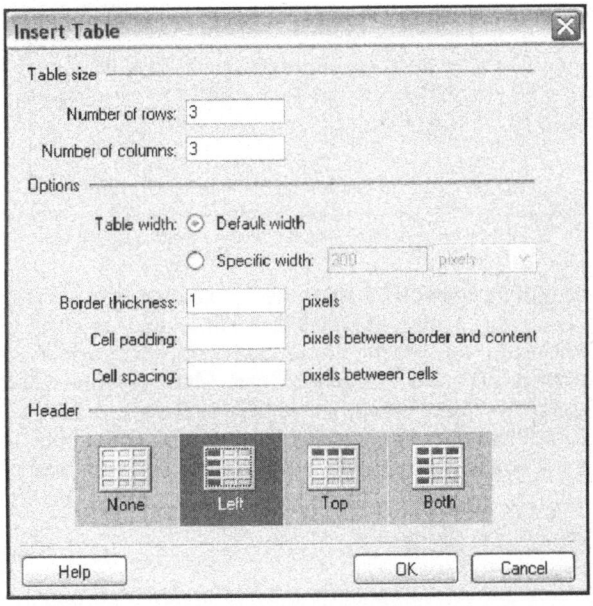

Choosing table scope using the Insert Table dialog box.

From this dialog box, users can choose to insert headers in the leftmost column, the topmost row, or both. If a user selects *Left*, Contribute writes each header cell as `<th scope="row">`. If the user selects *Top*, Contribute writes each head cell as `<th scope="col">`. This information helps alternative devices to accurately read the content of a table.

Using the following table as an example, Contribute writes each header tag as `<th scope="row">`. This associates each content cell with its appropriate header, so the screenreader will output, "*The Iliad, Used, $12.00*", instead of reading by column or "*The Iliad, The Stranger, Quo Vadis, Used, Used, New...*" and so on.

The Iliad	Used	$12.00
The Stranger	Used	$11.00
Quo Vadis	New	$18.00

An accessible table created in Contribute.

Accessible Templates

When it comes to ensuring accessibility, the most important thing you can do as the web site administrator is to first make sure your Dreamweaver MX templates are accessible. Dreamweaver MX includes several features to help you create accessible templates, and even update older templates to conform to accessibility guidelines.

Bold and Italic Code Options

Checking this option forces Contribute to use `<strong>` and `<em>` tags instead of `<b>` and `<i>` tags.

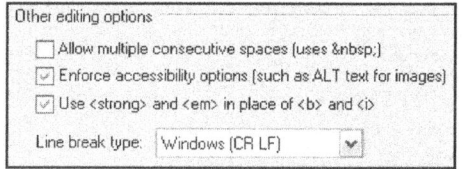

In this dialog box you can also choose to make users style bold and italic text with <strong> and <em>, rather than the deprecated <b> and <i>.

There's no visible difference between these tags – both `<strong>` and `<b>` create bold text as their default style, while `<em>` and `<i>` create italic text. However, `<b>` and `<i>` are deprecated in HTML 4, and using `<strong>` and `<em>` is recommended as an accessible alternative. These tags have semantic meaning – emphasis and strong emphasis. Many screenreaders will speak with emphasis when they encounter a `<strong>` or `<em>` tag. Bold and italic are purely visual tags that carry no semantic meaning, and therefore cannot indicate that text should be read with spoken emphasis. This change will be transparent to your Contribute users, who will only see the *B* and *I* buttons.

Set Permissions for New Pages

Contribute makes it easy for you to control the types of new web pages that a user can create. You probably won't want Contribute users introducing their own pages without restriction because you would inevitably have to check all new pages for design consistency, integrity of code, and other factors. With Contribute, you set permissions that determine the kind of pages users are allowed to create.

To set permissions for new pages, click on the *New Pages* category of the *Permission Group* dialog box, as shown below:

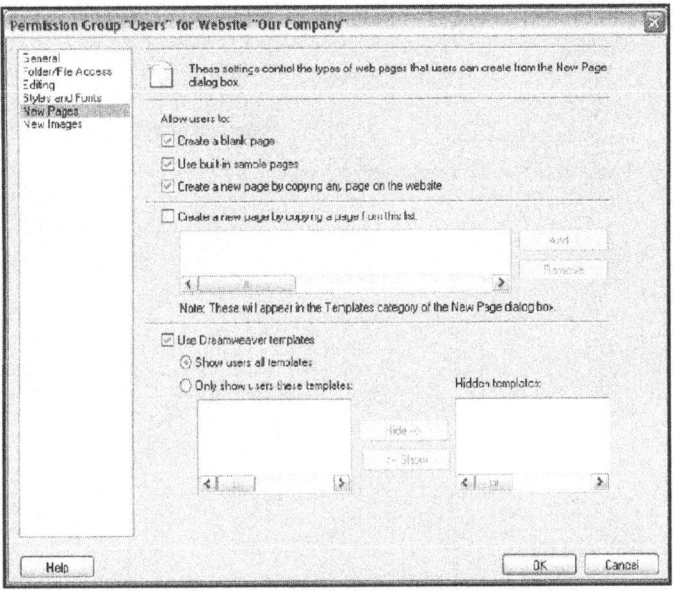

Setting the ways in which users can create new pages.

If you want to prevent users from creating new pages from scratch, uncheck the *Create a blank page* option. Allowing users to create pages from scratch practically defeats the purpose of web site management with Contribute.

Another option, *Use built-in sample pages*, allows users to create new pages based on a collection of sample templates that come with Contribute. Some of these templates may be useful, such as the calendar or presentation templates, but you'll probably want to restrict users from using the sample page designs within your own design. Or, you can selectively delete the templates you don't want them to use.

To protect the design, style, and code integrity of your site, you should choose from the remaining options:

- **Create a new page by copying any page on the website:** With this option, you can at least guarantee that your existing design and styles will be intact when a user needs to add a page to the web site

- **Create a new page by copying a page from this list:** With this option, you can use the *Show* and *Hide* buttons to create your own list of approved pages that users can choose from. Clicking the *Show* button will add a template to the list, and the *Hide* button removes a selected template from the list

- **Use Dreamweaver templates:** This option allows you to make available any Dreamweaver templates you have set up for your web site. You can set this option to show or hide specific templates from your collection. This is perhaps the best option because you'll have more control over the kind of page that users can create, and the regions on the page that users can edit

With the above options selected, users who click the *New Page* button will be presented with the dialog box shown below:

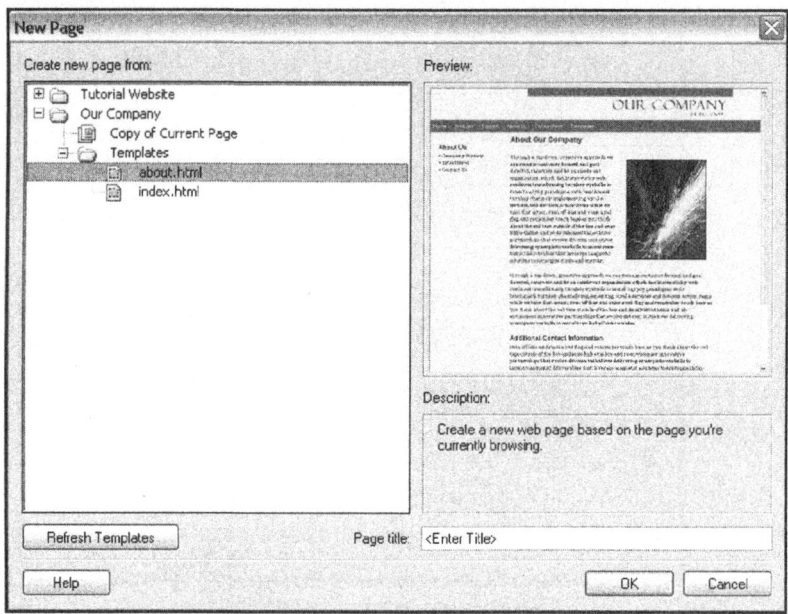

The New Page dialog box, including Preview screen.

The *Preview* pane makes it easy for Contribute users to scan through the templates you make available and select the page they wish to build from. With this feature, you can ensure that your contributors help to grow and improve upon your web site without having to worry about compromising your design, content, or coding standards.

Set Permissions for New Images

Your Contribute users may not have the experience to understand the importance of image file size on the web – that a large image can destroy a page's load time. Contribute makes it easy to set a limit on the file size of images that users add to web pages. Click on the *New Images* category of the *Permission Group* dialog box to set your desired limit.

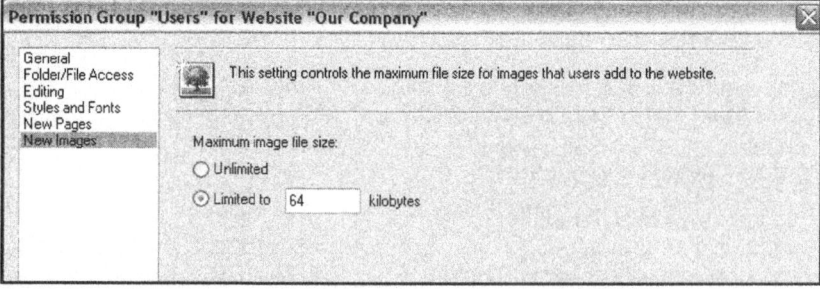

Setting the maximum file size allowed for user-inserted images.

The size limitation is set to 64 kilobytes by default, but you can change this value by entering a new value in the *Limited to* field, and clicking *OK*. Setting a size limit for images can help ensure that the pages your users edit will meet your standards for download time.

Create and Display a Style Guide

Your users will benefit from having a copy of your web site's style guide on hand as they work. Contribute provides an easy way to customize the *How Do I...* panel on the left side of the Contribute interface, as shown below (we saw how to do that in *Chapter 4*.)

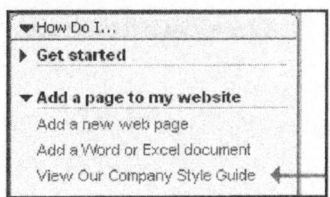

A good tip for your Contribute setup: add a style guide to the How Do I... panel.

With a style guide on hand, your users can easily reference the purpose and appearance of the styles you make available in the *Style* menu. If you create a web page that provides examples of each custom class that you create, your users will be more efficient and accurate when they edit web content.

In your `Tasks` folder (`%CONTRIBUTE%/Configuration/Content/Tasks`), you will see several HTML files named `Task2.htm`, `Task3.htm`, and so on. These pages appear in the *How Do I* section when you click on their corresponding links. You can use any one of these pages as a template for your style guide, or you can create your own from scratch. (Be aware that the *How Do I* frame has a limited width, so make sure you don't set any fixed widths.)

Summary

In this chapter, we explored many Contribute features that make it easy to establish, enforce, and maintain your web site standards, including:

- Enforcing your coding conventions
- Enforcing your style conventions
- Customizing the Contribute interface
- Ensuring conformity with accessibility guidelines
- Controlling new content parameters

Following the guidelines in this chapter will help you to ensure that your Contribute users always work within the style, content, and accessibility parameters that you establish.

6

In this Chapter

- Selling Contribute to your users and management
- Training users
- Supporting Contribute

Author: Lyn Wall

Soft Skills

Successful use of Contribute depends on the planning and support you provide. The successful webmaster will remain involved every step of the way, from how they present the use of Contribute to their users (be they customers or co-workers), to ongoing support. In this chapter, we will discuss:

- Selling Contribute to management
- Selling Contribute to users
- Training users
- Supporting Contribute

Selling Contribute

One thing that you can be sure of is that, every time you want to implement or even test a new application or technology, management will want a detailed and valid set of business justifications for taking on the expense of purchasing and implementing it. You may also have potential users that are afraid to learn new technology, or unwilling to invest the time needed to learn it. How are you going to get everyone to agree to use Contribute?

How are you going to get everyone to agree to use Contribute?

Selling Contribute to Management

Explain to management what Contribute's purpose is and find out if it fits in with the goals of the workgroup. It is not a scaled-down version of Dreamweaver MX; it is a totally different product. Contribute is a tool to allow workgroup members to modify site content without affecting the design of the site.

Explain the many benefits of adopting Contribute throughout your workgroup to management, as follows:

- Advantages over expensive content management systems
- System requirements
- Workflow
- Enforcing standards- and Accessibility-compliance
- Permissions-based system enhances security
- Dynamic pages
- Efficient resource-saving system
- "Mistake-proof" rollback mechanism

Explain the many benefits of adopting Contribute throughout your workgroup to management.

Now let's look at each of these benefits in a little more detail.

Advantages Over Expensive Content Management Systems

Contribute has distinct differences from CMS systems, which tend to be expensive and cumbersome to maintain, especially for small companies and sites. Compared with CMS systems, Contribute:

- Costs less to purchase
- Takes less time (and usually money) to implement
- Is cheaper to maintain
- Requires less user training

System Requirements

Contribute will work on Windows operating systems as early as Win98SE, and on Mac OS operating systems. For workgroups running Windows 98SE or better, no additional hardware is required to enable users to use Contribute.

Workflow

The workflow will depend on the dynamics of the organizations and departments involved. However, perhaps more importantly it will depend on how well you have configured the site and Contribute to meet the needs of your clients, and how well you have trained your users according to this book.

Compare your current workflow to add content to your site to the new workflow that will be used once Contribute is in place. Let's assume you have a very simple workflow for adding a new page to your web site. A typical workflow might look like this:

1. Marketing department creates new content for page

2. Page content is shared with webmaster

3. Webmaster creates page

4. Webmaster provides preview of page to marketing department

5. Marketing department requests changes

6. Webmaster modifies page

7. Webmaster provides preview of page to marketing department

8. Marketing approves page

9. Webmaster publishes page and creates the appropriate links to it

Now let's look at what the likely workflow would be under the Contribute system:

1. Marketing department creates new content for page

2. Marketing department creates new page in Contribute

3. Marketing publishes page

Not only do we have fewer steps, but the marketing department didn't need to consult the webmaster in order to publish a new page! The marketing department may have its own internal approval process, but that seemingly would add the same number of steps to each workflow option.

Does this mean that you, the webmaster, will have no involvement? Of course not – management counts on you to ensure that standards and practices are adhered to. You will probably need to review the site daily to ensure practices and standards are met, and that nothing happens to threaten its integrity. You will provide feedback to the contributors to help them improve their practices. You will be involved, but you will not be an obstacle to progress.

Enforcing Standards- and Accessibility-Compliance

If management is interested in compliance with both W3C standards for writing code and Section 508 Accessibility standards (which they should be in this day and age for many reasons, legal, moral, and practical), they will be pleased to know that Contribute can be configured to enforce many of these standards.

W3C standards are important because as time goes on, browsers are increasingly designed to render web pages based on these standards. To ensure that your design will render properly in future versions of browsers, they should conform to the W3C standards. Some organizations, such as government bodies, are required to adopt the Section 508 Accessibility standards, which provide primarily for the visitor who is visually impaired, including those visitors who use screenreaders. *Chapter 5* discusses these standards in more detail.

Contribute also can be configured to enforce internal web design standards and styles through the use of CSS stylesheets and Dreamweaver MX templates. For more on templates, see *Chapter 7*.

Permissions-Based System Enhances Security

Management is often concerned with security, so it is important that they understand that you can tailor the site to meet their concerns. You can separate users into groups that have permission to only edit files they need access to. You can further assure them that the FTP passwords you share with the users will be encrypted, meaning that you have no need to share the actual password. Assure them that in an environment that requires changing passwords on a regular basis, you will take responsibility for distributing updated connection keys.

If you were to set your users up with an HTML editor and FTP program for sharing updates to the site, you would not have the same level of security offered by Contribute. The connection key itself can be password-protected and communicated to the user separately. This allows for an extra measure of security, as you must have the connection key file and know the password in order to set up the connection. For more on Contribute security, see *Chapter 2*.

Dynamic Pages

Dynamic web pages created with ASP, PHP, or other dynamic languages have their background code protected – Contribute can only edit the HTML elements of a dynamic page, not the dynamic code. And Contribute doesn't offer direct access to the actual HTML code of a page. There is an option to allow a user group to edit scripts and forms, but this is turned off by default, and turning it on is discouraged. For more in using dynamic pages with Contribute, see *Chapter 9*.

Efficient Resource-Saving System

Management will be happy to hear that Contribute enables content providers to make changes quickly and will be very interested in the reduction in support and training costs compared to more expensive, complicated CMS systems.

"Mistake-proof" Roll Back Mechanism

Management should be concerned about backup plans. What happens if something goes wrong? What is to prevent a user from making changes that are later found to be incorrect? This is where the rollback feature of Contribute comes in handy. Contribute can save up to 99 rollback versions of each page, depending on the space you allocate to this function. The preview feature allows you to check that you are rolling back to the intended version.

Selling Contribute to Contributors

The chances are that most users will jump at the chance of being able to modify portions of the web site they directly contribute to, but they may also have concerns. They may be intimidated by learning a new application, or worry that they need to know HTML in order to edit web pages. They may wonder what happens if two people want to work on the same page at the same time. We'll address all of these issues in the following sections:

- Contribute's simple interface
- User workflow
- Check In/Check Out

Contribute's Simple Interface

You can assure your users that not only is Contribute going to be easy for them to learn, but you will be there to train and support them as they learn. The interface is similar to many word processing programs, so it will be easy to adapt to. They can even do all of their typing and editing in Word or Excel and import that content just by dragging the text into Contribute. The *How Do I...* panel is available to give them instant help when it is needed.

Most users will jump at the chance of being able to modify portions of the web site they directly contribute to, but they may also have concerns.

Let the users know that they do not have to worry about causing problems with the functioning of the web site. You will be setting up the site by assigning them to user groups with specific permissions. They will not be able to edit any web pages or code that they should not have access to. This is especially true if you take advantage of Dreamweaver's template functions.

User Workflow

Explain the workflow to your users in terms they can understand. Assure them that they will be able to concentrate on content, without needing to learn HTML. It takes just a few quick steps to make changes to the content, without needing to consult the webmaster:

1 Browse to a page

2 Edit the page

3 Publish the page

Check In/Check Out

Contribute ensures no two users can edit the same page at the same time, using the same Check In/Check Out feature as Dreamweaver. If you are editing a page and another user tries to edit it, they will receive a message saying that the page is not available for editing, similar to the one shown here:

> ⚠ You can't edit this page now because User (user) <user@mycompany.com> is currently editing it. Please contact <user@mycompany.com> for assistance.

A simple error message to inform users when another user is editing the page they are trying to edit.

Conclusion

Both management and content contributors will find that the improved workflow offered by Contribute is a big plus, and appreciate the fact that it can be configured to prevent people unfamiliar with HTML code from corrupting the operations of the web site. A strong selling point for management is the low price tag for installation and use compared to expensive content management systems.

Soft Skils

6

Training Users

Your users will require some training, whether it's one-on-one or in a group. Remember that to some of them HTML will be a big mystery, so it's important to discuss even the most basic concepts in terms they can understand. You also need to convey to them that they are not expected to take over the web design process, merely contribute content to the site. The time you invest in training your users will pay off in reduced support calls later on. Recommended topics for your training session(s) are:

Contribute Setup

- Setting up connections
- Contribute preferences
- Accessibility for Contribute users

Editing pages

- Exploring the Contribute workspace
- Creating new pages
- Writing content for the Web
- Browsing and navigating to pages
- Working with draft pages
- Explaining Check In/Check Out
- Editing Dreamweaver template-based pages
- Working with tables
- Working with images
- Working with hyperlinks

Contribute Features

- Working offline
- Designing for Accessibility standards
- Limitations & issues
- Previewing pages
- E-mail review
- Publishing pages
- Rollbacks
- Where to find help

The first thing you should do is provide each of your users with a printout of the *User Guide* that we're providing as a companion to this book, available for download along with the sample code at *http://www.glasshaus.com*. This guide is designed to cover what the users need to know, in a language they will understand.

As you cover these topics with your users, make sure to include any customization you have added and keep the permissions assigned to each group in mind. Also, discuss the standards you have for web site consistency. Hopefully you've set up CSS styles and templates to manage consistency, but make your users aware of the need for it as well.

As well as being covered in the *User Guide*, most of these topics have been introduced already in this book – below, we will go through each topics in a bit more detail, providing references to other areas of the book where appropriate.

Contribute Setup

First, let's look at the training topics for Contribute setup.

Setting Up Connections

For many, the biggest obstacle to using Contribute will be connecting to a web site. Contribute's connection key feature is designed to simplify the task of getting your user connected to the web site. Make sure you have thoroughly tested the key and communicated the password (if there is one) to each user.

Walk your users through the process of launching Contribute and importing the connection key.

Even if you are giving the user one-on-one training on their own PC, they should learn how to import the key because parameters may change and you may need to send them a new key. Show them how to delete an existing connection key so they can import any updated keys you give them. It's worth the time you take to walk them through all of the functions of the *My Connections* dialog box.

This material is covered in more detail in *Chapter 2*.

Contribute Preferences

Walk your users through their options by showing them *Edit > Preferences...* Explain each option and include your own recommendations. These options are covered in *Chapter 4*.

Accessibility for Contribute Users

If you have users with special needs, there are a number of ways to accommodate them. We already discussed how to enable Contribute to work with screenreaders in *Chapter 4*. Contribute also supports the Windows high contrast setting and follows most common Windows methods for navigating the workspace and dialog boxes using keyboard shortcuts.

Editing Pages

Next, we'll look at the training topics for editing pages in Contribute.

Exploring the Contribute Workspace

Go through each section of the workspace with your users:

- The Browser/Editor
- Sidebar
- Toolbars

Show them the opening window they will see when they start Contribute and explain the use of the Browser/Editor. Point out the sidebar, where the top is used for navigating open pages and the bottom *How Do I...* panel is a great resource for getting instructions on how to perform the tasks that are described there.

Point out that there are different toolbars for Edit and Browse modes. Later on, you can go into more detail about the buttons on each type of toolbar. Some of the more complicated functions provided in the workspace are looked at in *Chapter 3*; the more simple functions are self-explanatory.

Creating New Pages

Show your users how to create new pages. Take into account the user group permissions – what options they have for creating new pages. Emphasize the right way to create links to new pages on your site so that they don't create orphaned pages.

Writing Content for the Web

Writing content for the Web is different to writing for other media. It's a good idea to discuss some of the basic concepts with your content providers. This topic is too big to cover in great depth here, but some basic principles to review with them are:

- Be succinct – avoid rambling sentences
- Use consistent formatting
- Don't underline content unless it is a hyperlink
- Avoid writing wholly in capitals
- Use bulleted lists to break up large blocks of content and lists of hyperlinks
- Break long sections down into multiple pages that link to each other to minimize scrolling and shorten loading times

It's important that you review the conventions in use on your site with users (for example, if you consistently put book titles in italics rather than quotes) – make sure they understand the importance of maintaining consistency across the site.

Browsing and Navigating to Pages

Walk your users through the process of browsing to a page and clicking the *Edit Page* button, as well as how to select a page by selecting *View > Choose File on Website...* Keep in mind that everyone has their own way of working that is comfortable to them. Show both methods for choosing a page to edit and let the user choose the method they feel most comfortable with.

Encourage your users to create bookmarks for pages they commonly edit. Show them that they can organize their bookmarks into folders, in a manner similar to Internet Explorer Favorites.

Working with Draft Pages

Explain how to save a draft page. Encourage your users to save their changes frequently, and show them how to save pages for later by selecting *File > Save for Later* (shortcut: *Ctrl-Shift-L*). Point out that the saved draft page will appear in the *Pages* panel, to be selected at a later time when they are ready to continue editing that page.

Your users will be pleased to learn that canceling a draft page is as simple as selecting it and pressing the *Cancel* (*Cancel This Draft*) button.

Explaining Check In/Check Out

If you're a Dreamweaver user, this topic may seem obvious to you, but it can only help to make sure that your users understand how Check In/Check Out works. This way, they will understand why they are unable to edit a page and whether they should contact you for help when they cannot, or wait for another user to finish working with the page.

Editing Dreamweaver Template-Based Pages

Using templates for your site gives you greater control over the pages your users edit. Point out to them that they will not be able to edit page elements that are defined by the templates. Show them that the cursor will change to a "forbidden sign" when their pointer is over a locked area of a template-based page, as seen here.

Forbidden sign.

Show them the difference in appearance between locked and editable regions (which are outlined in green); make sure you point out the editable areas they are responsible for besides content, such as page title and headings. Make sure they understand the icons that appear for repeating template regions and how to use them.

When you update templates on the site, you will need to tell your users to close down Contribute and reopen it, if they will be basing new pages on templates (future versions of Contribute will include a *Refresh Templates* button). Warn them there will beoccasions where the site will not be available for editing while you Check Out pages based on templates and update them and the templates they are based on.

For more on Dreamweaver MX templates, see *Chapter 7*.

Working with Tables

If your users are familiar with Microsoft Word or other word processing packages, they probably are used to working with tables. Inserting an HTML table into a page in Contribute is as easy as filling in the following dialog box (remarkably similar to how it is done in Dreamweaver MX):

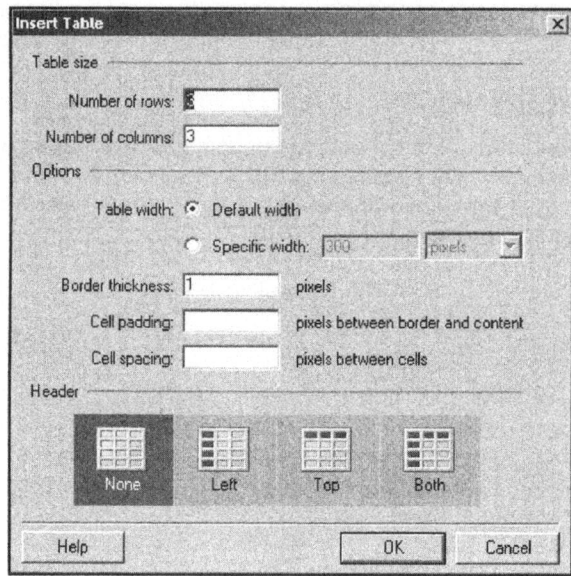

The Insert Table dialog box.

Walk them through the use of tables in Contribute, including these topics:

- Inserting a table
- Modifying the table's appearance
- Selecting table elements
- Resizing columns and rows
- Aligning text within table cells (you may have set up CSS styles for this)
- Cutting and pasting table elements
- Sorting data in tables

Working with Images

Most users will not be editing existing images or creating new ones, but they may wish to display available images on the page they are working on. It's a good idea to show them how to insert images both from their PC and from the assets available on your web server. Show them the three ways to insert images:

- Using the *Insert Image* button, or selecting *Insert > Image* on the menu
- Dragging an image from another source
- Copying and pasting an image into Contribute

Emphasize the need to add a descriptive name for the image to be included in the `alt` attribute of the `<img>` tag. This is a practice that is important for Accessibility and W3C-compliance. Encourage them to make sure that an image doesn't already exist on the site before uploading it, and tell them how to find and insert the existing image so they are comfortable with the process.

Give your users some guidelines for using images. Make sure they understand that images add to the load time of the page, so images should be used sparingly, and only if they are necessary. Show them how to use existing images on the site to avoid duplication of files on the server by uploading additional copies of images that are already available.

It's important for the users to understand that, when adding images from their PCs to the site, those images will be placed in a subfolder named *Images*, in the same folder the page resides in. If no such folder exists, Contribute will create it. *Chapter 3* discusses images in more detail, and *Chapter 5* discusses good Accessibility practices.

Working with Hyperlinks

Contribute does not handle links the same way Dreamweaver and other HTML editors do. Review the different options in the *Insert Link* dialog:

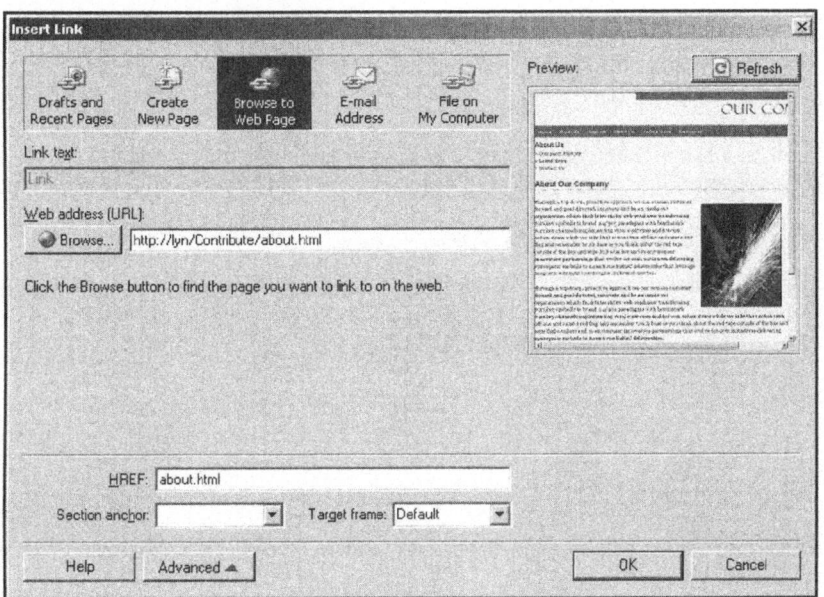

Inserting Hyperlinks in Contribute.

Show them the advanced features – they are really not all that advanced. They may want to be able to simply add a URL. Explain what a section anchor is – what we're used to referring to as a named anchor. Finally, show them how to create a link that opens in a new window by setting the *Target frame* in the *Advanced* section to *New Window*, but warn them they will not be able to open that page using Contribute's browser.

For more on hyperlinks, refer back to *Chapter 3*.

Contribute Features

Finally, let's go through the training topics for Contribute features.

Working Offline

It is possible to work on existing drafts even when no connection is available to connect to the web site. If Contribute cannot connect to your site or to the network, it will give you the option of working offline:

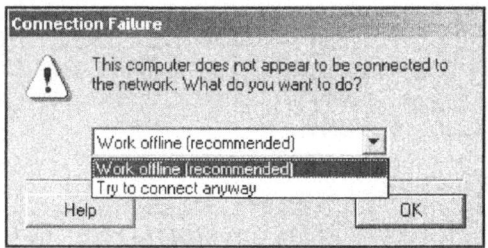

Working Offline When no Connection is Found.

Show your users how to toggle between online and offline mode using *File > Work Offline* on the menu. Point out that, even if they are working on a PC that is connected to the network or Internet, Contribute will continue to work offline until they manually switch back to working online.

Explain that they will be limited to creating new pages and working on existing drafts, and will not be able to browse to other pages or publish the page while they are working in offline mode.

Designing for Accessibility Standards

Even if your site does not strictly adhere to Section 508 Accessibility standards, we saw in *Chapter 5* that it is important to incorporate as many of the standards as possible. Review the standards with your users, and show them how to implement them.

You can enforce Accessibility standards for user groups in the editing section of the *User Groups Permissions* dialog. If you choose to do this, explain the implications when you train your users.

Limitations & Issues

There are several issues and limitations of Contribute that you may want to cover in your training session:

- **Frames**: If any of your pages uses frames or IFRAMES, discuss with your users how pages that use frames behave differently. Make sure they understand how to select a frame to edit and how to target frames using hyperlinks. There are some known issues with IFRAMES, especially in pages that contain multiple IFRAMES. You may find that you cannot enable your users to edit pages containing multiple IFRAMES

- **JavaScript**: Unless you have authorized the editing of scripts (which is strongly discouraged), make sure your users understand that there are scripts that they cannot edit. Also show them how to select a page to edit when the link to it opens the page in a new window (by choosing **View > Choose File on Website**, from the menu

- **Forms**: In most cases, users will not be able to edit `<form>` element properties

- **Invisible layers**: If you have any layers on a page with the `visibility` property of the `<div>` tag set to `invisible` when the page loads, the user will not be able to edit those layers

- **Office 97**: Office 97 documents cannot be dragged into the Contribute workspace. You can still copy and paste content from Office 97 documents into Contribute

- **Page Size**: Large pages may take a long time to load after clicking the *Edit* button

- **Single Quotes:** Have your users avoid using single quotes in URLs. They do not render properly in the Contribute browser

- **Formatting**: Some formatting may be lost when you insert Microsoft Word or Excel documents into a page. Users should be cautioned to review the inserted content for desired formatting

Previewing Pages

Show your users how to preview their files while in Edit mode (by pressing *F12*, or choosing *File > Preview*). This is important because there are cases where the page won't look exactly the same in Edit view as it will in the browser. To aid learning, relate it to the *Print Preview* your users are used to taking advantage of before they print word processing and spreadsheet documents. Contribute's internal browser uses the Microsoft Internet Explorer browser engine. It is a good idea to show your users how to preview pages in Netscape, Mozilla, and any other browsers used by a significant percentage of the visitors to your site.

E-mail Review

Walk your users through the e-mail review process. There will be occasions where they'll want to show a colleague a draft page before publishing it. Let them know what to expect. You can find more about the e-mail review facility of Contribute in *Chapter 2*.

Publishing Pages

Make sure your users feel comfortable with the entire process by showing them what happens when they click the *Publish* button. Remind them that any links they create will need target pages.

RollBacks

Users always want to know what will happen if they make a mistake. Show them how easy it is to roll back to a previous version of a published page. Contribute also creates previous versions of any images that you edit by launching the external image editing application through Contribute. For more on rollbacks, see *Chapter 2*.

Where to Find Help

Make sure your users are familiar with both Contribute's *Help* menu and the information available in the *How Do I...* panel. Highlight areas where help is available for the tasks they will be performing most often and include a review of custom sections you have created for the *How Do I...* panel. This will encourage them to find answers on their own before they call you for help.

Supporting Contribute

The success of your rollout of Contribute to users depends on:

- How your site is structured
- How you have configured Contribute
- How well you train your users
- How well prepared you are to support your users

In *Chapter 2* we talked about site definitions. In *Chapter 4* we looked at the customization options available to control the permissions and include custom documentation within the Contribute *How Do I...* panel and Welcome page. Finally, in *Chapter 5* we discussed best practices for a successful Contribute site.

In this section, we will discuss:

- Taking Advantage of Contribute's Extensibility
- Documentation
- Common Support Questions & Known Issues
- Maintaining your web site

Taking Advantage of Contribute's Extensibility

If you can, take the time to learn about the customization features discussed in *Chapter 4*. If you take advantage of this extensibility to produce a customized Contribute environment that is tailored more to your users needs, your effort will pay off in reduced support calls and a higher comfort level for your users. Make sure to incorporate your customizations into any training sessions and materials you present to your user groups.

Documentation

Training your users is an important step towards a successful Contribute project. However, it's just as important to provide documentation resources that your users can refer to before they call you for help. If your workgroup is comfortable with hard copy documentation, create a reference for them that complements the training session. The *User Guide* we're providing as a companion to this book (downloadable from the glasshaus web site) should act as a good resource for your users to refer to.

Also, take advantage of the ability to customize the *How Do I...* panel to provide a reference for common tasks and questions, as shown in *Chapter 4*.

Common Support Questions & Known Issues

Even after the most thorough preparation and training, your users will have questions when they sit down to work with Contribute, especially for the first time. Below we provide an FAQ to help answer some of the more common questions and issues that may come up, along with possible solutions.

Why Won't My Connection Key Work?

Usually, connection key problems are caused by either permission or proxy server problems.

Configure any directory where the users may be editing pages to allow read, write, and modify permissions. The method to do this will depend on your web server's operating system.

If your user will be connecting through a proxy server, you must create the connection key using the same proxy server or it will not work on your users' machines. The reverse holds true as well. If you are connecting through a proxy server but your user is not, the connection key you create will not work for them.

Why Do My Pages Look Different in Edit Mode?

Contribute does a good job as a WYSIWYG HTML editor. However, if the page you are editing has links to stylesheets that are created using JavaScript, the styles will not render properly in the editor.

Why Can't I Create a New Page?

If you haven't given the user's group permission to create new pages, that is the cause. Otherwise, check the permissions on the server to make sure they have read, write, and modify permissions for the folder they are trying to create files in.

Why Can't I Edit My Page?

Usually pages are locked because another user is editing the page. If you determine this not to be the case, you can use your FTP client to delete the matching `.lck` file for that page; the user will then be able to edit it.

If a page is based on a nested template, all levels of that template page must be present on the server in order to edit the page.

Contribute cannot edit pages where server-side includes include the `<body>` and `<html>` tags. They must reside in the document itself.

Why Are Some Tags Highlighted in Yellow, and Why Did I Get an Error Message Saying There Was Invalid Code When I Opened the Page to Edit It?

Contribute detects invalid HTML code and notifies the user. If there is a problem with the code on the page, you should check it yourself, visually or using a validator, and make the necessary corrections.

6

Why Does the Page Open in My Browser Instead of Contribute?

This occurs when a link's target is set to open the link in a new window. In order to edit the page for that link you need to use *View > Choose File on Website* from the menu. You can also copy the URL from the default browser window and copy it into Contribute's browser to open the page.

Contribute Crashed!

If the user is trying to edit a page that contains a Flash movie, Contribute may crash if they haven't got the right version of the flash Plugin installed. Have them upgrade to the latest version of Macromedia Flash Player.

Why Isn't My Mouse's Scroll Wheel Working?

Contribute works best with Microsoft IntelliMouse driver; even if the mouse you are using isn't an IntelliMouse, installing these drivers should solve the problem.

The Contribute Browser Window Keeps Resizing When I Open Pages!

If a custom JavaScript on the page modifies the window dimensions, it may cause the Contribute browser to resize as well. In this case, the user will have to manually resize Contribute to correct the problem.

The Browser is Displaying a Save Box, What Do I Do?

This can happen when you browse to a Microsoft Office document. Tell the user to click *No* to close the dialog box. If you click the *Edit* button prior to clicking within the document, this problem will be prevented.

Why Doesn't the Contribute Browser Work the Same Way as Other Browsers?

Some pages won't work in the Contribute browser. Specifically, many online shopping carts do not function properly and you may be unable to log into password-protected web sites using the Contribute browser.

Maintaining Your Site

No matter how carefully you've configured your Contribute project you are still an integral part of the maintenance of your site. Set up a schedule to review your site for consistency, compliance with W3C, and Accessibility standards as necessary. For instance, when text is dragged from an Office document, single and double quotes are not converted to character entity codes. This can result in pages that are not W3C-compliant at best, and at worst, interfere with scripts located on the page. Regular review will allow you to fine-tune the changes made by your users.

As we mentioned earlier, templates require special treatment. Whenever you update templates, you must notify your users after you upload the new versions. This is because currently Contribute only checks for new template versions at startup. Future versions of Contribute should include a *Refresh Templates* button. Also, make sure you check out all pages based on your template before updating those pages, otherwise they will not be updated when you make changes to the templates they are based on.

Summary

In this chapter we have discussed some of the issues that will come up when you are working with users and management towards a successful Contribute project, either when you are trying to get your managers and users to agree with you about what a good idea implementing Contribute would be, or when you are preparing to support your Contribute users after implementation. Specifically, we have looked at the following topics:

- Selling Contribute to management
- Selling Contribute to users
- Training users
- Supporting Contribute

Soft Skils

6

7

In this Chapter

- What are templates?
- Creating templates
- Associating templates with different permission groups

Author: Michael D. Hazard

Using Templates In Contribute

Contribute is designed to integrate with Dreamweaver MX templates. By basing your site on Dreamweaver MX templates you will help to ensure design consistency across your site, as well as making modifications across your entire site much easier. If you do not use Dreamweaver MX, you can still take advantage of template functionality, although you will need to create your templates by hand, instead of using Dreamweaver MX's WYSIWYG interface. In this chapter we will look at:

- **The advantages of designing a site using templates**: We can use templates to lock down portions of a page, quickly update all pages within our site based on a template, and so on. Contribute users cannot modify templates, and are therefore forced to comply with the design standards set forth in the template

- **Creating templates in Dreamweaver MX**: Since Contribute recognizes templates created in Dreamweaver 4, there will be some discussion of templating functions in previous versions of Dreamweaver. However, the focus is placed on Dreamweaver MX templates because they are much more powerful and flexible than Dreamweaver 4 templates

- **Creating templates with applications other than Dreamweaver MX**: Dreamweaver templates use HTML comments to control web pages. Since Dreamweaver MX templates use standard HTML, you can create templates in any application you want, from GoLive to Notepad

- **Various ways of optimizing your site structure for using templates**: This includes using Contribute's administration features to associate templates with permission groups. Depending on how your site is structured, you may have more than one templates folder. If this is the case, then you must define multiple sites in Dreamweaver MX and/or Contribute

What Are Templates?

A Dreamweaver MX template is a unique web file that is created by web professionals and used by content developers as a base for new web pages (it could be called a page skeleton). Like any web page, a Dreamweaver MX template may contain CSS styles, server-side code, and links to images.

Typically, web professionals create templates in Dreamweaver MX. Templates are saved with the .dwt file extension to a templates folder in the root of a web site. Once the template files are saved to the templates folder, they are available to content developers using Contribute, who can then create new pages based on the templates, in much the same way that Microsoft Word users create new pages based on templates. Like Word templates, Dreamweaver MX templates are a separate file type. A content developer creates a new page from the .dwt file and saves it as an HTML file (or other common file format, for example ASP or PHP). They do not save the new page as a .dwt file. New pages created from templates contain no proprietary code because Dreamweaver MX templates use standard HTML comments to manage pages.

Templates are created in the same way you would create a typical HTML page. You design your page layout, and add images, includes, tables, and so on. Once you've finished the page, you mark sections of the page, called **editable regions**, as places where content developers can add content.

In the example below, the company graphic, header, navigation, and footer are placed on the page by default. Whenever a content developer creates a new page based on this template, these objects are automatically placed in the page. In this way, templates cut down on the time required to create a new page because common page elements are included automatically, and this also helps to keep the design of your pages more consistent. In addition, when a template-based file is saved, all links are updated so that they point to the correct location. Therefore, end users do not have to update links to images and other files because Dreamweaver or Contribute handles the task for them.

When creating a template, you can specify what regions of a page can be edited. As a web professional using Dreamweaver, you can create and edit template files. Contribute users cannot create or edit template files. They can only create new HTML pages based on templates.

The non-editable regions of the page are referred to as being **locked down**. When a portion of a page is locked down, content developers cannot edit the section's content (their cursor will turn into a "forbidden" sign if they try to mouse over locked-down sections). They cannot add or delete content from locked regions either through Contribute or Dreamweaver MX.

You can extend the concept of locking down sections of your page by adding repeat regions and optional regions to your templates. Repeat regions enable you to control how content is added to a page. For example, if a repeat region is used on a table row, content developers can add additional rows to the table but only add the type of content to these rows dictated by the repeat region. You can apply repeat regions to other objects on the page, for example, HTML lists, but tables are one of the most common examples of their use you'll meet.

Another important new feature in Dreamweaver MX is nested templates, which allow for different levels of updating ability on pages created from these templates. Dreamweaver connects all pages based on templates with the original template file.

Therefore, if you add a new image to the locked header of a template for example, you are prompted to update all the pages based on that template. This makes managing pages very easy. Editable regions, nested templates, and repeat regions are not the only templating features you'll find in Dreamweaver, but we don't have the space to discuss them all in detail in this chapter, so here we'll just stick to these, the most widely-used three.

7

The more advanced template features you might want to explore as you become more comfortable with templates are listed below:

- **Editable Attributes**: Sometimes you won't want to give content contributors the ability to add content to a page as allowed by a standard editable region. There are times when you simply want content contributors to only be able to modify the properties of an object on the page. You can choose to use editable attributes in such a situation. Editable attributes give content contributors the ability to edit a tag's attributes, for example, change the background color of a table but not edit the content of the table

- **Optional Regions**: Optional regions allow you to denote portions of a template as optional. Optional regions can be used to turn content on or off, or they can be used to give content contributors the ability to choose between different content. For example, if our support team creates tech notes about products and each tech note contains one of three images denoting the importance of the information on the page, we can create a template in which they can choose which image to use. We would place all three images into the template, and apply the optional region to each image. Content contributors who create a new page based on the template can then use the *Template Properties* dialog box to turn each image on or off

- **Parameters**: While not exclusively used with optional regions, parameters can be added to a template to programmatically control optional regions. For example, we can create a template which will be used by our support team to create tech notes. Instead of having the support team manually choose which image to use in their tech notes, as described above, we could have them rank the tech note on a scale of 1 to 10, with 1 being less important and 10 being high importance. Our tech support content developer would then use the *Template Properties* dialog box to enter the number from 1 to 10, and the template would decide which image to use based on the value entered into the parameter

Parameters are extremely powerful. Because they're based loosely on JavaScript, you can use them to create content programmatically. The power of parameters comes at a price – they can be difficult for first-time template developers to understand. Therefore, it's recommended that you explore parameters only after you become comfortable with the basic templating features discussed in this chapter.

As you can see from the information above, Dreamweaver templating is robust. It is also quite complex, and because of this, only the basics of Dreamweaver templates will be covered in this chapter. For more information on Dreamweaver templates, refer to the Dreamweaver manual (find it online at http://www.macromedia.com/support/dreamweaver/documentation.html).

The Drawbacks of Templates

Templates are a very good tool to use when working with Dreamweaver and Contribute. However, there are some drawbacks to using them.

If you're working in an environment where designers and developers use multiple tools to edit content, Dreamweaver templates might not be as useful. While Dreamweaver uses HTML comments to identify sections of a template, the code is only recognized by Dreamweaver. If you open a template-based page in GoLive or FrontPage, the locked regions will not be enforced. GoLive and FrontPage will treat the Dreamweaver template code as nothing more than a standard HTML comment. While this doesn't cause direct problems, it does mean that you cannot force users of the other tools to conform to the template page layout.

There are other problems encountered when using Dreamweaver templates in an organization that is not standardized on Macromedia tools. While you can create templates in any HTML editor by simply typing in the Dreamweaver HTML template comment codes, the process is difficult. In fact, if you're planning on using some of the more advanced template functions such as repeat regions, nested templates, and so on, it's pretty much a requirement that you own Dreamweaver. We'll briefly explore manually creating basic templates later in this chapter, but it is strongly recommended that you purchase Dreamweaver if you're planning on using templates.

The screenshots in this section are taken from Dreamweaver MX. Dreamweaver MX supports many new and powerful templating features that Dreamweaver 4 does not. While Contribute recognizes Dreamweaver 4 templates, you should consider upgrading to Dreamweaver MX to take advantage of the new templating features. Contribute does not recognize templates created in versions of Dreamweaver prior to version 4.

Another potential problem you may run into when using templates is resistence from content developers within your organization. One of the reasons to use templates is to ensure consistency across your web site. If your site does not enforce consistency now, trying to move to such a model can be difficult. As a web professional, you know that consistency in design and navigation is important, but convincing others can be difficult. It's important that you take the time to explain to content contributors that consistency is not about limiting their creativity, but rather a way to make your site easier to use.

One last problem you may encounter when using templates is their occasional quirkiness. What do we mean by quirkiness? Simply put, there are times when you'll receive less than helpful error messages when using templates. It's important that you test your templates before you allow content developers to work with them. If you discover an error, you may want to switch to Code View because seeing the code that makes up your page will make diagnosing the problem easier.

It's important that you test your templates before you allow content developers to work with them.

Dreamweaver MX has a command, *Check Template Syntax* (located in *Modify > Templates*), that will verify that your template markup is error-free – you can only use this command on a .dwt file. While you should run this check, you should also test your templates manually. The first step in checking your template is to create new documents based on your templates and verify that there are no tags highlighted in yellow in Design View, which indicates errors. The second step is to add content to the page, work with all the template features, and save the document. After you've created a document or two based on your template, open the template file, modify it, and update the pages based on the template. If you don't encounter errors, then your template is ready to distribute to content developers. The time you spend testing your templates is nothing compared to the time you'll spend on support if end users encounter error messages when using templates, and republishing your pages after you've fixed the problem.

Templates and Contribute

Templates work no differently in Contribute than they do in Dreamweaver. Content developers can use templates to base new pages on, and the template interface in Edit mode is the same as that of Dreamweaver. When creating templates, you have access to all the new Dreamweaver MX template features listed overleaf:

7

- Editable regions
- Repeat regions
- Optional regions
- Template parameters
- Editable attributes
- Nested templates

The only difference between Dreamweaver's template features and Contribute's template features is that you cannot create or edit templates within Contribute. In addition, some CSS-based designs trip up Contribute in Edit mode, as we'll see later on in this chapter.

Creating a Template

It's not required that you strip out all changeable content. In fact, you may want to include filler content in the template that contains examples of some of the styles used in your design. However, you should remove unnecessary content such as images. Including such things might confuse your end users.

The first step in creating a template is to design your page. If you have already written a web page, and you'd like to use its design as a template throughout your web site, open it in Dreamweaver then strip out any content the page might contain, just leaving in the common elements. Next, add editable regions to it as necessary, using the information below as a guide, before saving it as a template and deploying it on your site.

In this example, we'll be creating a template with a table-based layout for our example *Our Company* site. Creating templates from sites with CSS-based layout is similar to creating table-based templates. There are, however, some problems with the way Contribute renders CSS-based pages in Edit mode. These problems are discussed in detail in the note below.

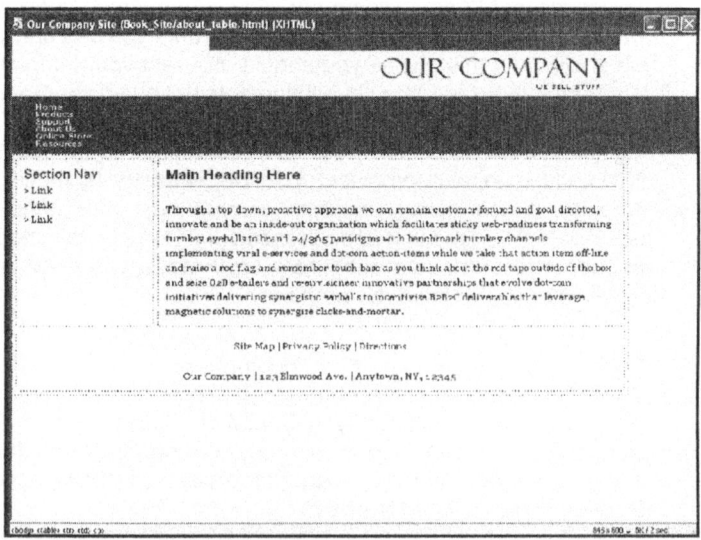

The stripped-down layout used as the starting point for our template. Note that we've removed the links from the section navigation and populated the content area with dummy text.

A Note on CSS-Based Layouts

CSS-based design can cause problems in Contribute, as seen in the examples below. In this example, we've created two ids, mainleft and mainright. The ids are defined as relative and their positions are defined in the stylesheet. While the page renders fine in Browse mode, the page design is destroyed in Edit mode, so severely that content developers cannot edit the page. The code for laying out the page is listed below, along with a screenshot of how the page looks to content developers while working in Edit mode.

```
#mainleft {
   margin-top: 28px;
   position: relative;
   padding-left:20px;
   background:#F4F0E4;
}

#mainright {
   position: relative;
   top: -92px;
   line-height:130%;
   width: 500px;
   left:200px;
   background:#F4F0E4;
}
```

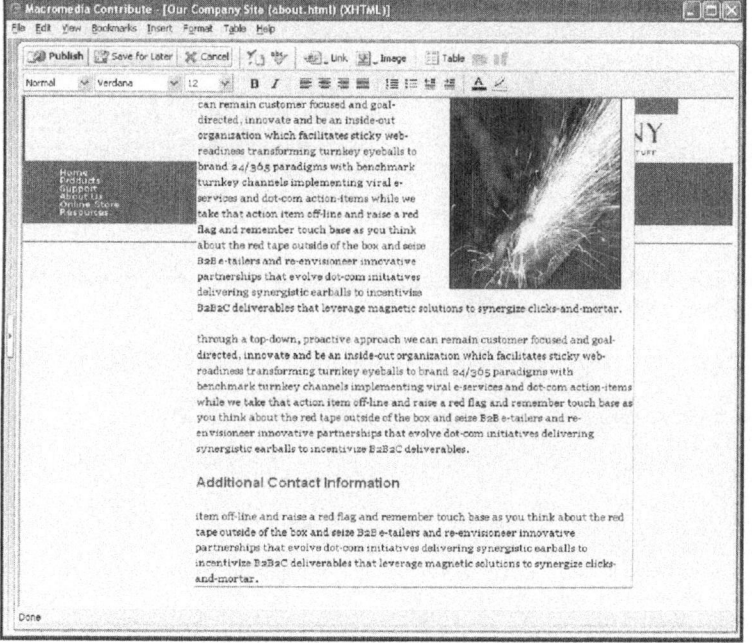

Some CSS-based layouts fail to render correctly in Contribute's Edit mode. The above example is so bad that the page is un-editable in Contribute.

The Dreamweaver Design View still chokes on the CSS, but at least you can edit the page content. Keep this in mind when designing your pages if you're using CSS for layout: You cannot trust the Design View in Dreamweaver. You should test your designs by opening them in Contribute. While Dreamweaver and Contribute share a similar code base, there is enough of a difference for testing to be important.

The same page as the previous example, only now it's displayed in Dreamweaver. It is editable in the Dreamweaver Design View, but not in Contribute, so make sure you test your templates thoroughly.

There is no simple solution to this problem. If your site uses a similar method to lay out pages, consider floating your `ids`, as seen here:

```
#mainleft {
   float:left;
   padding-left:20px;
   width:240px;
   background:#F4F0E4;
}
#mainright {
   margin-right:10%;
   margin-left:250px;
   max-width:600px;
   background:#F4F0E4;
}
```

By changing our stylesheet, we've solved the problem, as seen in the following screenshot. While having to design for compatibility with Contribute might not be ideal, taking it into account provides a passable solution: it works, and your design is still CSS-based. You have the best of both worlds.

Another solution is to use tables instead of CSS. Of course, this is not the modern preferred way of designing a page, although most current sites use tables for layout. If you're going to use tables, remember to keep them simple. Try to avoid multiple nested tables if possible.

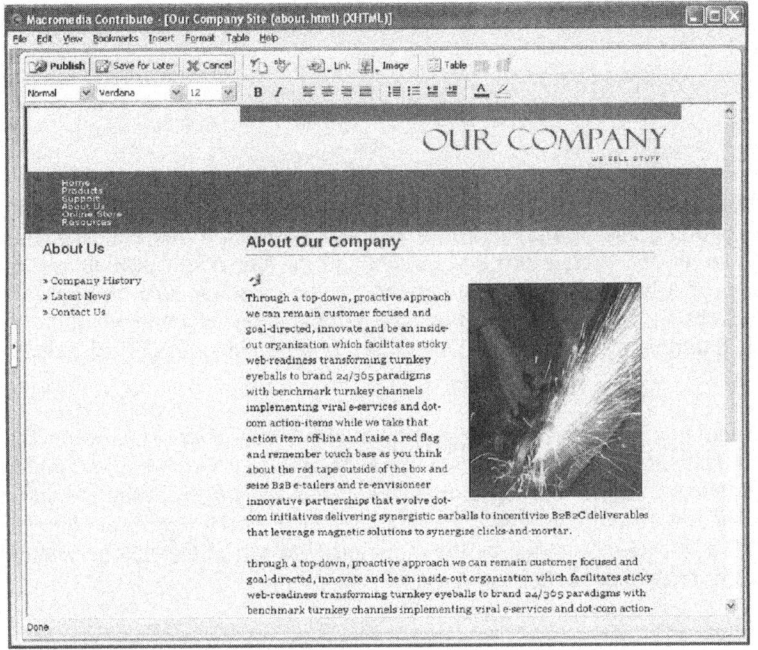

By changing our ids to float, we're able to maintain a CSS-based design while ensuring compatibility with Contribute's Edit mode.

Editable Regions

As noted above, an **Editable Region** within a template is an area that can be changed when creating a new page based on the template. If an area is marked as editable, content-developers can add any type of content to the region – images, tables, lists, and so on. Editable regions are the most commonly used templating feature, and are typically applied to table cells, table rows, or other areas within a page that will hold the page's main content. Therefore, when creating a template, you select page elements, for example a table row (`<tr></tr>`), and make it editable. Anything not marked as an editable region is locked. The *Our Company* site will contain two editable regions: the main content area and the navigation area.

The *Our Company* site contains five sections, and each section will have its own template. If you're using Dreamweaver 4 to create your templates, you will be required to create five separate templates, one for each section. If you need to update content that is locked on each template, for example, change the header image, you will need to update each template in order for the changes to cascade down through your whole site.

However, if you're using Dreamweaver MX, you can use nested templates to better manage your files, as we shall learn more about in the next section. We'll assume you're using Dreamweaver MX since, unlike Dreamweaver 4, you can use it to manage Contribute sites.

When you create a template in Dreamweaver, the page title and meta data tags are automatically set as editable regions so that users can modify these values.

In the following examples, we're using a table-based layout. If you used CSS, you'd select the appropriate `<div>` and apply the editable region to it. If you've created layers using Dreamweaver's Draw Layer tool, you should select the layer and apply the editable region to it. Users will then be able to move the position of the layer. If you don't want your users to be able to do this, apply the editable region within the `<div>`, and not to the `<div>` itself.

Nested Templates

Nested templates allow you to create new templates based on other templates. There are many advantages of doing this. Templates make site management much easier because you can quickly update objects across your entire site by editing one file. When you update the content within a locked region of a template, all pages based on the template are also updated. When you nest templates, updating the parent template (the template on which other templates are based) will cause all child templates to update, which in turn updates all of the HTML pages based on the child templates.

The *Our Company* site contains five sections: *Products*, *Support*, *About Us*, *Online Store*, and *Resources*. Each section shares a common header image, site navigation, and footer. Using nested templates enables us to define the global portions of the page (portions that will be locked on all pages), and allows us to create five child templates based on the parent – one for each section. That way, the site will still be controlled by the main template whilst the nested templates define the look and feel for the individual sections in the site.

Content developers should only be given access to the templates that are required for them to do their job.

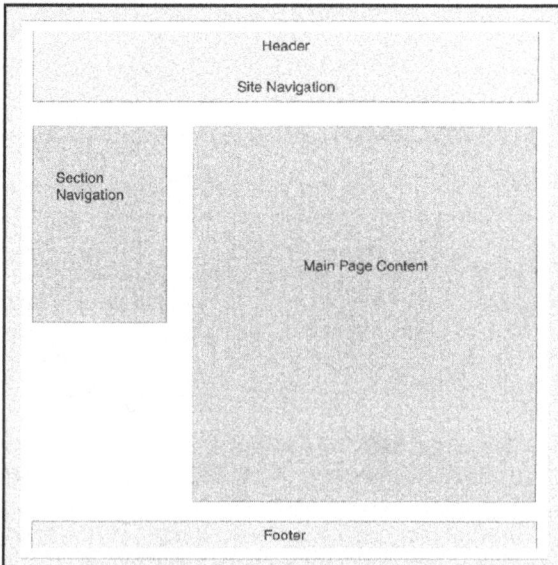

The header, site navigation, and footer are shared on all pages, and should therefore be kept locked on all pages.

Our section templates (child templates of the above parent) will each have different section navigation. The navigation title will be locked on each child page, but we'll allow users to add links to the navigation. Content developers will create new pages based on the section (child) template. Since we're able to hide templates from chosen permission groups in Contribute, you should always hide your parent templates – content developers should only be given access to the templates that are required for them to do their job. In our example, the parent template is used simply to make managing the site easier. We do not intend to base HTML pages on it.

Note that templates control only the non-editable (locked) regions of a page, and not the editable regions. Updating text within the parent template's section navigation will not update the text within the child templates. However, updating locked content (for example, changing the header image) will update the child pages because the header section is locked.

Creating the Parent Template

To create the parent template, you simply need to create your editable regions then save the file as a template.

First, open up one of the pages of our sample site. We then need to select the areas that we want to make editable. It's a good idea to do this by clicking on the relevant tag in the tag selector at the bottom of the Document window because it's easy to select the wrong area of the actual page display.

For example, we want to make the entire content table cell editable; therefore, we'll select the `<td>` tag in the Document window. Keep in mind that since we've selected the `<td>` tag, users can edit the cell's properties. If you don't want content contributors to be able to edit the cell properties, simply create an editable region within the cell, rather than using the cell itself.

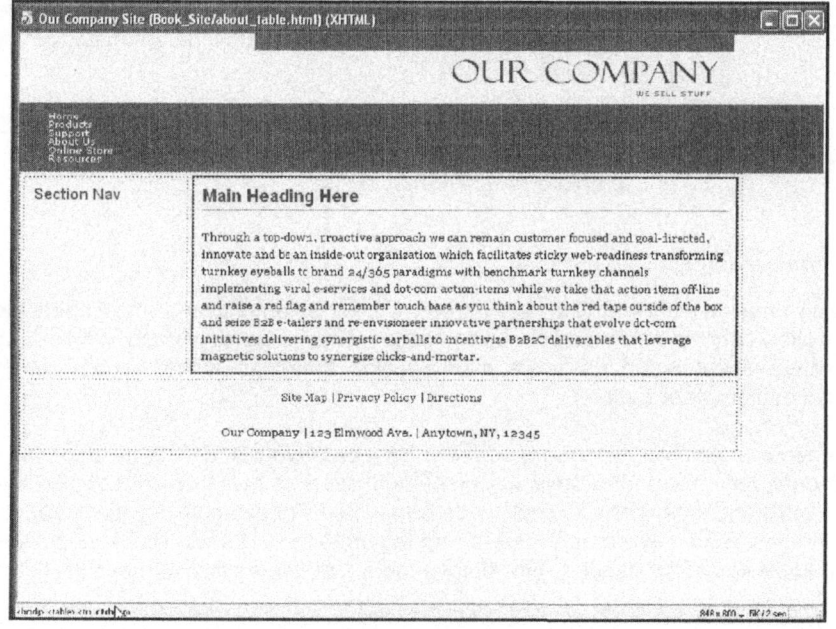

We've selected the <td> tag in the Document window. Notice that the entire table cell is outlined. We'll make this editable.

Next choose *Insert > Template Objects > Editable Region.* You'll also be prompted to give the region a name. You should give the region an easily understandable name because users will see this name when they create new pages.

Click *OK* after you've named your region, and you will turn the main content area into an editable region. We'll also create an editable region for the section navigation – the process is the same: select the table cell containing the navigation and make it editable. You will notice that a tab and a highlight box are added to each table cell, as seen here:

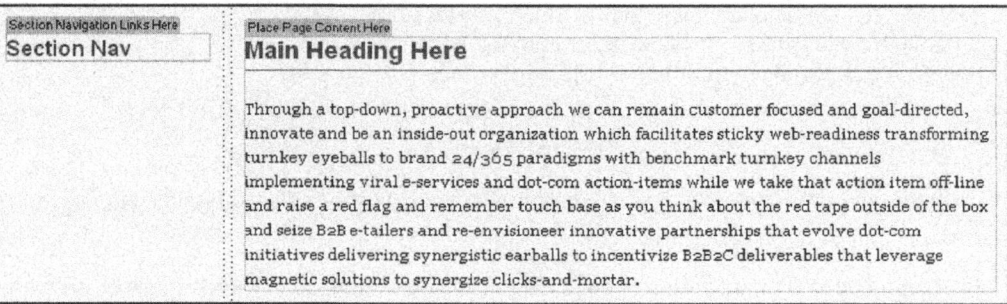

The parent template contains two editable regions. Note that both regions have been given easily understood names.

If you do not create editable regions in a template, Dreamweaver will warn you that the document does not contain them. It does this because a page without editable regions cannot be edited by content developers.

Now verify that the template syntax is correct by choosing *Modify > Templates > Check Template Syntax.* Once of the more frustrating aspects of working with Dreamweaver MX templates is the fact that the template tools are located in two different places within the menu system. However, there is an extension that fixes this problem – for more information, visit *http://www.dwfaq.com/* and search for the Template-Lover's Suite. This extension costs a mere $6, and groups the template tools together, saving you time.

Lastly, save the file by choosing *File > Save As Template.* Since this is the parent template on which we'll base our section templates, we'll name the template *parentTemplate.*

Repeat Regions

Before we create a child template, let's introduce another template feature: **Repeat Regions**. Repeat regions allow users to easily add content to pages. They're typically used with lists and tables. When you create a repeat region, users are given a toolbar that enables them to add, remove, and reorder elements in the repeat region.

Repeat regions give you even more control over a site layout because, by enforcing the structure of tabular data, they make it harder for content developers to mess up your design. As users click on buttons within the toolbar, the region's code is modified. For example, if you wanted to set an ordered list as a repeat region, you'd apply the repeat region to the `<li>` tag. Users would then click the plus (+) to add list items, the minus (–) to remove them, and the arrows to move list items up and down.

The repeat region toolbar as seen by content editors. The toolbar is used to add, remove, and change the order of repeated regions.

Creating the Child Template

To create a child template, you need to follow these steps:

- Create a new template based on another template
- Modify the template as needed
- Create any new editable regions
- Save the file as a template using a different name

Now let's look at creating a child template in more detail.

Repeating tables are so common that there is a Repeating Table tool that you can use to more quickly create repeating tables, by setting up the table and the repeat region within the same dialog box. We're not using this tool because we want to show how to create repeat regions for other HTML objects such as lists. Both the process described below and the Repeating Table tool work for creating repeated tables, however, you'll probably want to use the Repeating Table tool because it's faster (find it under Insert > Template Objects > Repeating Table).

Create a new document based on the parent template – we will base all section templates on this file. Note that only the sections we unlocked in the parent template are editable here – the navigation and content areas.

The Navigation Menu

In the left table cell that contains the section navigation, change the *Section Nav* title to *Products*. Insert a one-row, one-column table into this cell, and set the cell padding to 5, the cell spacing to 0, and the border to 0. Set the width of the table to 100%. This table will contain our navigation links. Our users will repeat the table row to add additional links.

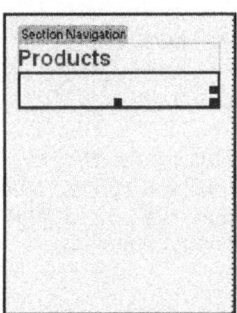

We've added a table to the left cell.
This table will contain our links.

Next, add dummy *Link* text to the table cell we just created and give it a dummy target of #. Style the link text with the `sectionLink` CSS class (found in `basic.css`, in the CSS folder of our site) to make it fit in with the look of the rest of the page.

7

We will now turn this hyperlink-containing table row into a repeat region. Select the `<tr>` tag from the tag selector and choose *Insert > Template Objects > Repeat Region*. You are prompted to give the region a name. Choose an appropriate name such as *Navigation*.

Now select the `<td>` tag and insert an editable region – you must insert an editable region if you want users to be able to edit the content of the table cell (a repeat region only enables the table's row to repeat). While at first this extra step may seem unnecessary, in reality it allows for a lot of flexibility when you design templates.

Simply put, we're adding an editable region within the repeat region so that our content developers can add and edit content within the table cells they add.

Our navigation region should now look as follows:

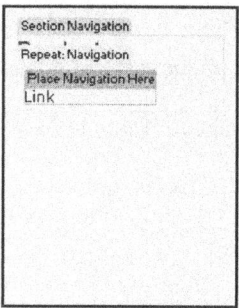

Now we've made our table into an editable repeat region, so our users will be able to add new links to the menu as required.

All that remains to do now is give the editable region a name, for example, *Place Navigation Links Here*.

Test the template syntax by choosing *Modify > Templates > Check Template Syntax*, then if it is fine, save this new template as *Products*. You've created a nested template. The *Products* template is based on the parent template we created earlier.

You can now create additional templates for the *Support*, *About Us*, *Online Store*, and *Resources* sections, following the same method outlined above. Once we have a set of nested templates that are based on a single parent template, we can change non-editable regions within the parent template and update all of the nested, child templates.

Testing a Template

Now that we've created our templates, we should test them. As stated earlier, it's a good idea to test your templates in Contribute since your end users will use Contribute to create content, and the way that the temples appear in Contribute can differ from how they appear in Dreamweaver. Since our page is laid out with tables, there shouldn't be any problems, but testing is still a good idea. Occasionally you may find that users cannot add content to an editable region. This is usually the result of applying the editable region to the wrong HTML tag.

To test a template, first open Contribute and begin editing your site. Choose *File > New Page* to display the *New Page* dialog box. Under the *Templates* folder, a list of the templates you've created is displayed. Depending on how you've set up your site, you'll have numerous options listed in this dialog box. For example, depending on the way you've set permission groups, content developers may be able to create a blank web page or a new page based on a copy of the current page. However, content developers can only save new pages to the folders where they have edit permissions.

Select your template. A preview of the page is displayed. Give your page a title and click OK. Remember that Dreamweaver automatically creates an editable region in the head of the document so that users can edit the page title and meta data.

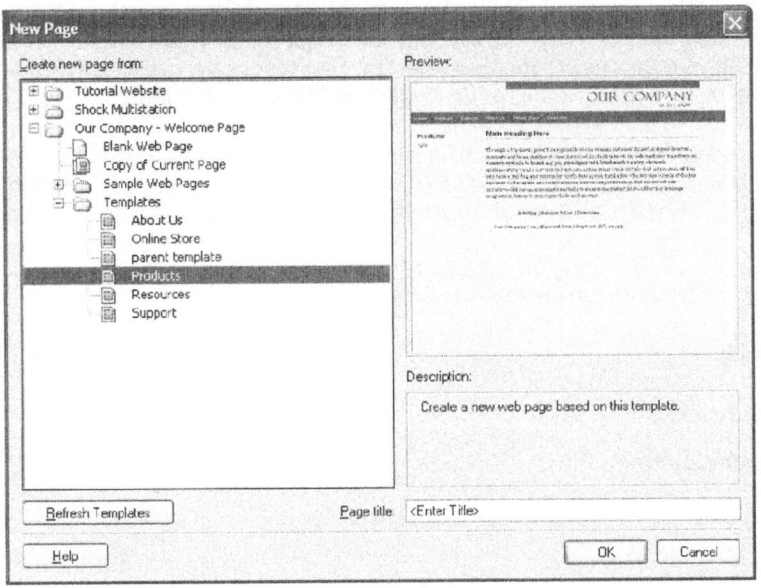

Creating a new web page based on your template in Contribute.

Add links to the navigation section by clicking the plus sign. Change the names of the links and reorder them by using the up and down arrow keys. If no error is displayed, and you're able to modify the text in the way you expected, your templates are working. Note that the navigation title, *Products*, is not editable even though in our parent template it was. This is the result of nesting the template and adding the additional editable region to the child template.

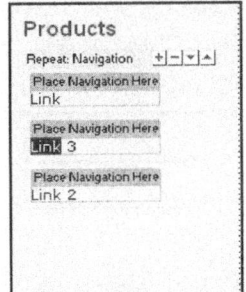

Editing our navigation menu in Contribute.

If this all went OK, your templates are working correctly. If you receive an error, or an option didn't work correctly, return to Dreamweaver and fix the mistakes. Of course, you should also test your designs in other browsers and on various platforms.

Creating Templates without Dreamweaver

You can use Contribute to edit content on sites that were not created in Dreamweaver. Virtually all of the functionality is available when you do this except templating. You can, however, create templates in other applications – any HTML/text editor really. That said, the process is tedious and error-prone. If you plan to create templates by hand, consider using a good HTML code-editing software package such as Homesite on the PC or BBEdit on the Mac.

As stated earlier in this chapter, Dreamweaver templates use HTML comments to designate regions as editable. You can write these comments in any application you want, from Homesite to GoLive. If we look at the code used to create an editable region, we will see that the region starts with

```
<! - TemplateBeginEditable name="someName" -->
```

and ends with

```
<! -  TemplateEndEditable -->
```

Repeat regions start with

```
<!-- TemplateBeginRepeat name="someRegion" -->
```

and end with

```
<!-- TemplateEndRepeat -->
```

Between the start and end comments is your HTML, as seen in the example below:

```
<table width="100%" border="0" cellspacing="0" cellpadding="5">
  <!-- TemplateBeginRepeat name="Navigation" -->
  <tr>
    <td class="sectionLink">
      <!-- TemplateBeginEditable name="Place Navigation Here" -->
      <a href="#">Link</a>
      <!-- TemplateEndEditable -->
    </td>
  </tr>
  <!-- TemplateEndRepeat -->
</table>
```

Note that the repeat region starts before the table row and ends after it, and the editable region is contained within the table cell. If you stop to think about it, this makes sense. When we add a navigation link, we're repeating the table row, but the content is placed within the table cell.

Dreamweaver template syntax is a very complex topic, and is beyond the scope of this chapter. Refer to the Macromedia web site for more information. Macromedia make most of their product manuals available in PDF format, and the Dreamweaver MX documentation contains information on template syntax. You should also visit the templating section of the designer and developer center on Macromedia's site at http://www.macromedia.com/desdev/topics/templates.html.

When creating a template in an application other than Dreamweaver, remember to add editable regions around the `<title>` element, as seen in the code below. Dreamweaver automatically does this when you create a template, but you'll need to do this manually if you're not using Dreamweaver.

```
<!-- InstanceBeginEditable name="doctitle" -->
<title>Our Company Site</title>
<!-- InstanceEndEditable -->
```

The name given to the editable region should be `"doctitle"` and the `<title>` tag must be placed within the region.

You can't change page properties such as body color, text color, and so on because Contribute tries to add these to the `<body>` element. Since the `<body>` element is not contained within the editable region, you cannot change these attributes. The only option available to content developers from within the Contribute *Page Properties* dialog box is *Title*. This is true for both Dreamweaver-created templates and manually created templates.

If you plan to write templates in another application, it is even more important that you test your templates before making them available to users. There are many template features in Dreamweaver MX, only a few of which have been discussed in this chapter, and it's very easy to make mistakes when using some of the advanced features. A mistake in a template can lead to data loss; it will certainly lead to phone calls from content developers who are receiving errors in Contribute.

When you've completed work on a template, you must save it to the `Templates` *folder located in the root of your site. Contribute looks for site templates in this folder. If it's not saved there, Contribute may not find the template. In addition, remember to save the file with the* `.dwt` *extension.*

7

Dreamweaver Templates and Permission Groups in Contribute

Now that we've created a set of templates, we need to associate our templates with the Contribute permission groups who will make use of them. Conversely, we can hide templates from particular permission groups if we don't. For example, if our marketing department creates pages for the *Products* section of our web site, we can associate the *Products* template with the marketing department permission group, but hide the remaining five templates.

By default, Contribute also allows users to create blank web pages, create web pages based on built-in samples, and create web pages based on a copy of the page users are currently browsing. If you're concerned about maintaining consistency across your site, it's recommended that you disable these additional features and only allow users to create pages based on templates.

We looked at creating custom user groups in *Chapter 4*.

Associating Templates with Permission Groups

To allow certain user groups to only use certain templates to create pages in Contribute, follow the steps outlined here:

1   Open the *Administer Web Site* dialog for your site by choosing *Edit > Administer Web Site*, then your web site. In order to associate templates with permission groups you must be the site administrator

2   Select the permission group you wish to edit. In our site example, we'll edit the *Marketing* permission group

3   Click the *Edit Group* button

4   In the *Permission Group* dialog, select the *New Pages* option

5   Uncheck *Create a blank page*, *Use built-in sample pages*, and *Create a new page by copying any page on the website*. We're unchecking this last option because it allows users to copy any page on the site. For example, our *Marketing* group could copy a page from the *Support* section, which we don't want to allow

6   Make sure that *Use Dreamweaver templates* is checked. Even if you create templates in another application, as long as you save them to the `Templates` folder and use the `.dwt` extension, they're available for use in your site

7   Select the *Only show users these templates* radiobutton. By default Contribute shows all templates to all permission groups

8   Select the template you want to make available to our *Marketing* permission group from the *Hidden templates* list (they only need to use the *Products* template), and click on the ← *Show* button. The template is moved to the left textbox. Any template listed in this box will be available to the permission group

Your *Permission Group* dialog box should now look like this:

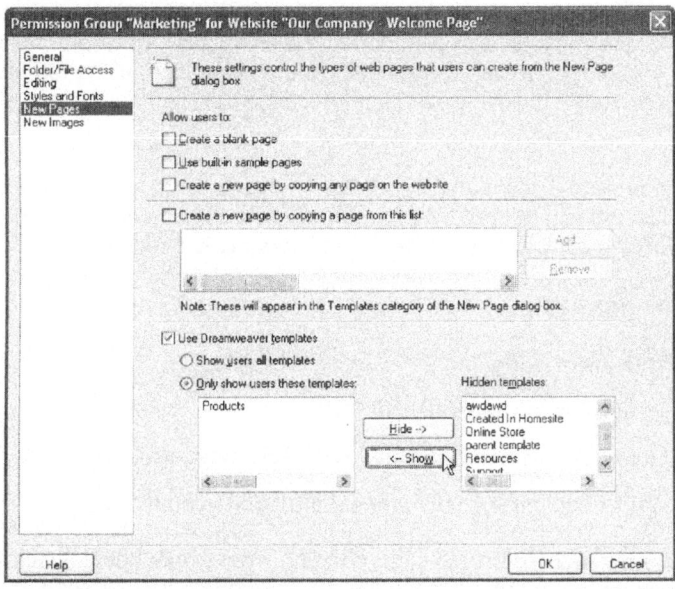

Setting up the Marketing group so that they can only create new pages from the Products template.

Click *OK* to save your changes. You can always make changes to the permissions later on if required. Now, when someone from the *Marketing* permission group creates a new page, only the template associated with that group is displayed, as seen below:

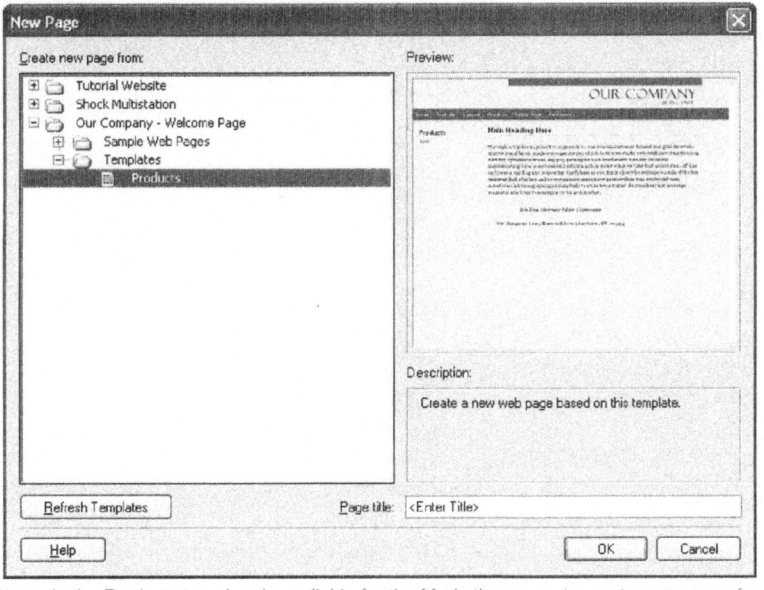

Now only the Products template is available for the Marketing group to create new pages from.

Summary

Using Dreamweaver templates with Contribute is a useful way for web professionals to ensure that content editors will conform to site design guidelines. In addition, using templates makes managing a web site much easier for the site's developer because they can quickly and easily update site-wide content.

Keep in mind though that templates can help you enforce design guidelines by making certain content uneditable, but you will not have full control over the content they create – you will still need to monitor the site regularly to make sure that its integrity is maintained.

In this chapter we explored:

- The advantages of designing a site using templates
- Creating templates in Dreamweaver MX
- Creating templates with applications other than Dreamweaver MX
- Various ways of optimizing your site structure for using templates

You should now explore the other features and find what works best in your situation. If you do not use Dreamweaver, you can still create templates for Contribute, but keep in mind that the process is much more difficult. If you're considering using templates and do not own Dreamweaver, we strongly recommended you purchase at least one copy, even if it's used just for templating.

8

In this Chapter

- Using Contribute to edit dynamic web sites through use of server-side includes

Author: Marc A. Garrett

Dealing with Dynamic Sites

Until now, we've used Contribute exclusively to work with static sites. What you may not know is that Contribute works well with dynamic sites as well, as long as you plan the site structure carefully and have realistic expectations of what Contribute can and can't do.

As you may know, the term *dynamic site* commonly refers to a web site made up of pages in which the content is pulled from a server-side datastore such as a database. A page sends a request to the database and the database returns a set of data to the page to be displayed on the client machine. This process is handled by an *application server*. Among other duties, the application server is responsible for processing requests from the client and handling connections to the database. In this chapter, we'll explore ways to use Contribute successfully with an application server.

Dreamweaver MX templates are a large part of creating pages with Contribute: templates generated in Dreamweaver MX interact smoothly with Contribute to allow the easy updating of static web content (for more on templates, see *Chapter 7*). While templates are a popular feature within the Dreamweaver MX community, many developers prefer to assemble dynamic pages using server-side includes.

Server-side includes (SSI) are pieces of HTML or other code that are stored in separate pages. When you wish to include these pieces of code in other pages, you refer to them using some kind of include statement (which varies depending on what server-side language you are using). These includes are handled on the web server, so the page is assembled before the browser ever sees it.

In this chapter, we will show you how to get the best of both worlds: we will work on a site using SSI, while still allowing your Contribute users to make site-wide updates to static content. In this chapter, we discuss:

- Understanding the difference between Dreamweaver templates and SSI

- Planning your site structure to support SSI and Contribute – both at the same time

- Configuring a Contribute site to support multiple permission groups and include pages

Software Requirements for This Chapter

Since we'll be working with an server-side scripting language, the requirements for running this chapter's code are a bit different from those for the other chapters in this book. In addition to having Contribute installed on your content editor's machine, to get the most out of this chapter, you will need:

- An operating system that supports a web server. Suitable ones include: Microsoft Windows 98, NT 4, 2000 (professional or server), and XP Professional, Mac OS X, and Red Hat Linux

- Microsoft Internet Information Server (IIS) or Apache Server (*http://www.apache.org*) installed on your production machine

- An application server environment, needed to process and serve your dynamic pages. The code in this chapter is written in JSP and was tested on a Windows machine with JRun4 (*http://www.macromedia.com/software/jrun/* – trial version available)

- The sample Microsoft Access database, dbContribute.mdb, found in the ZIP file located at this book's companion web site. Note that as long as you have a Windows machine with ODBC drivers installed, you do not need to have Microsoft Access installed in order to read the database via ODBC. In case you are using a Linux or other non-Windows machine for your server, I have also included two flat text files in the code download: tblEmployees.txt and tblUsers.txt. You can easily import these files into MySQL (see *http://www.mysql.com*) or the database of your choice

A note about server-side languages: debates over which server-side scripting language is "the best" typically involve as much unreason and vituperation as the Inquisition at its peak. I've chosen Java Server Pages (JSP) for the examples in this chapter because it can run on both Windows and Linux servers, and because you can run it with free software. I've also provided downloads written in ColdFusion and PHP, in case you prefer those languages. For detailed instructions on setting up the software needed to run these examples, please see the README *files that accompany the downloads available from http://www.glasshaus.com.*

- Macromedia Dreamweaver MX 6.1 installed on your development machine

- An image editor, such as Macromedia Fireworks MX, installed on your development machine

- The tutorial files. Download them from this book's companion site and unzip them into the root folder of your web site

The good news is that almost all of the necessary software listed above is either available as open source or as free time-limited trial versions, so you won't need to make any additional investments to run the code.

Of course, a full discussion of application servers and using Dreamweaver MX to build dynamic sites is beyond the scope of this book. If you'd like to learn more about the subject, check out a good book such as *Dynamic Dreamweaver MX* (*Rachel Andrew et al, glasshaus 2002, ISBN: 1904151-10-8*) or *Dreamweaver MX: PHP Web Development* (*Bruno Mairlot et al, glasshaus 2002, ISBN: 1904151-11-6*).

Why Not ASP or ASP.NET?

You may be wondering why I haven't included ASP or ASP.NET downloads for you to make use of as well. Well, I did start to write them, but I came across some interesting problems with them that you should know about. Contribute doesn't seem to handle ASP/ASP.NET includes in the way most people would want to develop ASP sites.

First, let's look at the ASP/HTML include format: `<!--#include  file="myPage.inc"-->`. The problem is that when you browse an `.inc` file, the web server doesn't parse the HTML; it just shows the mark-up like it was regular text. This means that if you want to let a Contribute user edit the `.inc` file, Contribute is going to show the mark-up, which is bad. To get around this, you can include an `.html` file instead of an `.inc` file, but most people don't actually work with includes that way.

Second, let's look at the ASP.NET include format: `this.Controls.Add(this.Load Control("mypage.ascx"));`. The problem here is that, by default, an ASP.NET server will not let you browse an `.ascx` file. Instead, it simply won't serve it and will throw an error, so Contribute can't open the `.ascx` include for editing. Again, you can work around this by including an `.html` file instead of `.ascx`, but ASP.NET developers won't want to give up the benefits of `.ascx` files.

Instead of including sample ASP and ASP.NET sites that include strange unconventional code, I'd encourage those of you who work with ASP or ASP.NET to experiment with your own solutions to these problems. Who knows, maybe they will be fixed in future versions of Contribute?

Configuring Your Machine for This Chapter

Once you've obtained the software listed above, you should take the following steps to prepare your work environment:

- Install an application server. We have suggested using JRun above, but you could also use Jakarta Tomcat (an open-source servlet container that you can download at *http://jakarta.apache.org/tomcat/*).

- Create an ODBC data source called dbContribute to connect to the Microsoft database dbContribute.mdb. If you're using Windows XP Professional, you can do so by choosing *Start > Settings > Control Panel > Administrative Tools > Data Sources (ODBC)*. In the ODBC *Data Source Administrator* dialog, click the *System DSN* tab. Click *Add*, choose *Microsoft Access driver (*.mdb)*, and click *Finish*. For *Data Source Name*, type dbContribute. Click *Select*, and browse to the location of the file dbContribute.mdb saved on your system

- Create a new Dreamweaver site called *Dynamic Contribute Site*. Set the root folder to /ch9, which you should have unzipped into your web site's root folder. If you prefer not to enter the site settings yourself, simply open Dreamweaver and import the Dreamweaver site definition file Dynamic Contribute Site.ste found in the folder /ch9/assets

Note that you can find installation details and links to help you troubleshoot your setup in the readme.txt *files that accompany the code downloads for this chapter.*

A Hypothetical Dynamic Site

Assume that you're responsible for building and administering the intranet of a small company. Your boss comes to you with the following requirements:

"I need you to spend less time making administrative changes and more time programming. Let's give the IT and the Human Resources departments the ability to make their own updates."

"No problem", you think, "this sounds like a job for Contribute".

On his way out the door, your boss throws a final curve ball, as expected:

"Oh yeah," he says, "let's make our web site like a portal, where each department claims a bit of space on the homepage for their information. And I need to have a searchable employee database. Make sure no one can muck up the pages you build, and protect the whole site with a password. Can you do that by tomorrow?"

At this point, you might *stop* thinking that it sounds like a job for Contribute!

Immediately, you can see two challenges with this scenario:

- Contribute sets permissions at the *folder* level, not the *page* level, let alone the *sub-page* level! Somehow, you must find a way to let users from the IT and HR groups make changes that show up on the portal page, while keeping one group from overwriting or changing the other's work.

- In order to put a searchable employee database on the web, you'll need to use an application server. Any sensitive code could easily be broken if a non-developer attempts to make changes. How do we protect it?

A Quick Walkthrough

Fortunately, we've already built the site for you. Open your web browser and browse to the server where you've configured the site, most likely *http://localhost/ch9/index.jsp*. You'll be confronted with a standard login screen. Provide a username and password to enter the site (unlike a real site, the usernames and passwords are provided on the menu of this login page). If you log in successfully, you'll see a very basic company intranet page, which allows you to view IT and HR announcements, as well as to search for employees. As you click through the different pages, note that each section has an identical layout; the only difference is the background color of the header – all other styles are inherited from a single stylesheet.

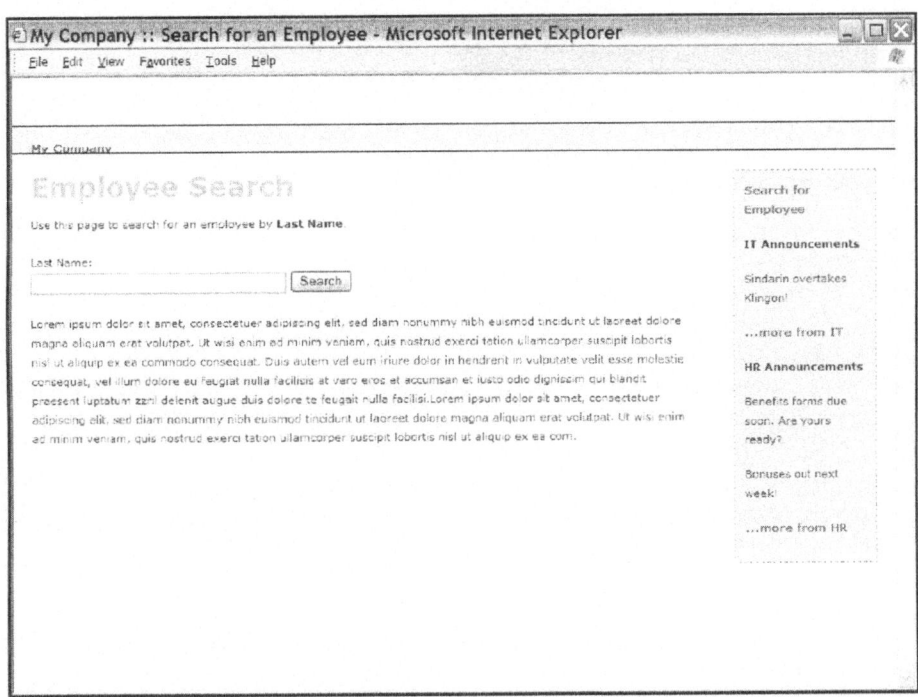

Your site visitors can search for an employee or read messages from the HR and IT departments.

Click *Search for Employee*. Type the name `Smith` in the *Last Name* input box and click *Search*. You will see several results matching the search. If you wish, you can also click within the menu to read announcements from IT and HR. It is these announcements that we wish to let the respective departments handle on their own.

Finally, note that the site is password-protected: if you attempt to access a page directly without logging in, you are redirected to the login screen.

All of the dynamic site features are basic functions built using the Dreamweaver MX menus. In other words, none of the site required hand coding. We'll spend the rest of the chapter looking at strategies to build this type of dynamic site and maintain it with Contribute. Let's get started.

Site-wide Content

Using site-wide content mechanisms such as SSI on your pages lets you reuse common code snippets such as navigation, headers, and footers – great for making template files and cutting down on file size.

Let's look at an example to demonstrate the power of site-wide content. Open the file `/ch9/portal/sample.jsp` with Dreamweaver MX or a text editor and study its code. As you can see, it's a simple page with three sections (it has no SSI): Content, Header, and Menu, as shown overleaf.

```
<%@ page contentType="text/html; charset=iso-8859-1" language="java"
import="java.sql.*" errorPage="" %>
<html>
<head>
  <title>My Company :: A Sample Page with No Includes</title>
  <meta http-equiv="Content-Type" content="text/html; charset=iso-8859-1">
  <!-- import a stylesheet --->
  <style title="text/css">
    @import url(../assets/styles/columnRight.css);
  </style>
</head>

<body>
  <div id="header">
    <a href="index.jsp" title="Home Page of Company Intranet">My Company</a>
  </div>

  <div id="content">
    <h1>No Includes</h1>
    <p><strong>NOTE: This page has no include files.</strong></p>
    <p>Page content would normally go in this area.</p>
  </div>

  <div id="menu">
    <p><a href="search.jsp" title="Search for an Employee">Employee
Search</a></p>
    <p><strong>IT Announcements</strong></p>
    <p>Sindarin overtakes Klingon!</p>
    <p>
      <a href="it.jsp" title="More announcements from the IT department">
      ...more from IT</a>
    </p>
    <p><strong>HR Announcements</strong></p>
    <p>Benefits forms due soon. Are yours ready?</p>
    <p>Bonuses out next week!</p>
    <p>
      <a href="hr.jsp" title="More announcements from the HR department">
      ...more from HR</a>
    </p>
  </div>
</body>
</html>
```

The stylesheet for this site is taken directly from BlueRobot's open source Layout Reservoir (*http://www.bluerobot.com/web/layouts/*). I've used CSS positioning to make the pages as simple as possible so we can focus on the content (CSS positioning allows you to place elements on a page without relying on tables for your layout). The contents of the Announcements menu reappear on each page of the site. This means that if the IT or HR departments change their minds about their announcements, you must edit each page of the site by hand and re-post the entire site.

That's a nuisance. A much better solution would be to use site-wide content for items common to many pages, thereby making it only necessary to perform such updates once. There are three common site-wide content mechanisms in use today:

- **Use Dreamweaver Templates:** Templates allow you to create fixed and editable regions of each page. With a template, you can ensure that new pages conform to the style and layout of existing pages. Although templates are an ideal solution for including common text in pages of a static site, they have some drawbacks. First, if you don't have access to Dreamweaver MX as your editor, it's almost impossible to make an emergency update on a common page element using templates. Second, when you do make your template changes, you have saved time by not having to make the same changes to every page on your site, but you still have to upload or re-publish every single page to your server before your users will see the change

- **Use a server-side include technology, like** `jsp:include`**:** These technologies include files from the server *as the page is served*. This has powerful implications: by including a file dynamically, you can change a single menu, upload it to the server, and instantly change the content of 500 pages. Although including files using SSI is vastly more powerful than using Dreamweaver templates, there are drawbacks here as well. Your organization must have the budget and expertise to develop and support a dynamic site. For a small static web site, adopting an application server might be overkill. Also, building the page dynamically each time it is served takes a bit more of your server's processing power than serving a static page. Some developers would argue this difference in speed could become noticeable on very high-traffic web sites. Finally, SSIs, unlike Dreamweaver templates, have no built-in way of keeping amateurs from breaking your design or your code

- **Store the data in a database:** Content management systems can store site-wide data in databases. Doing so allows you to automate updates to content easily and archive previous content. Content management systems are expensive to purchase, however, and building one requires server-side knowledge that many organizations may not have. For a small dynamic site, a fully-fledged content management system is unnecessary

In our sample scenario for this chapter, the boss has requested that you provide a searchable employee database and password protection. Since this requires that you use an application server such as JSP, PHP, ASP, or ColdFusion, SSIs make sense.

Let's return to the `sample.jsp` file: ideally, you should be able to store the menu, content, and header sections in site-wide files. Let's see how it's done.

Open `/ch9/portal/index.jsp` with Dreamweaver MX. On this page, the `<div>` elements look like this:

```
<div id="header"><a href="index.jsp" title="Home Page of Company Intranet">My
Company</a></div>

<div id="content">
  <h1>Welcome</h1>
  <p>
    Welcome to the My Company intranet. We currently have the IT and Human
    Resources departments online.
  </p>
</div>

<div id="menu">
  <jsp:include page="menu.jsp" />
</div>
```

Notice the change in the `menu <div>`. Remember that in `sample.jsp` the menu took up about ten lines of code. Here, those ten lines have been moved to a separate file called `menu.jsp`, which is now included on this page via a simple `<jsp:include>` tag.

All major server-side scripting languages provide a simple way to include common files. Here are the five that Dreamweaver MX supports, along with the code for including a file with each one:

- **ASP.NET**: `this.Controls.Add(this.LoadControl("mypage.ascx"));`. However, recall the problems mentioned earlier in the chapter with using ASP.NET includes with Contribute
- **JSP**: `<jsp:include page="myPage.jsp" />`
- **ColdFusion**: `<cfinclude template="myPage.cfm">`
- **ASP**: ASP does not support dynamic includes, but you can use a standard HTML include with the following syntax: `<!--#include file="myPage.inc"-->`. However, recall the problems mentioned earlier in the chapter with using HTML includes with Contribute
- **PHP**: `include("myPage.html");`

To understand the power of using SSI, open the file `/ch9/portal/menu.jsp`. Change the phrase *Search for Employee* to *Employee Search*. Save the changes and publish them to your server, and then browse to any page that includes the `menu.jsp` file. The text of the menu has instantly changed for all of the site's pages!

Now that you've seen how easy it is to update static text in a dynamic site, you should instantly begin thinking of creative ways to get other people to do this work for you. Let's plan the site for Contribute. Remember the essential challenge: find a way for people from different Contribute groups to edit data *on the same page* without being able to change content from another user group. Are you up to it?

Planning the Site Structure for Contribute

As it turns out, the skills required to plan a Contribute-friendly dynamic site are very similar to the skills you've already developed in this book's preceding chapters. Contribute doesn't deviate from the model of folder-level permissions. The trick is to give users access to content from their own folders, and then assemble that content into a single page.

As you learned in *Chapter 2*, flat site structures don't lend themselves to Contribute permission groups and can be difficult to maintain as your site grows. While there are many strategies for organizing your site folders, if you are building a dynamic site for use with Contribute, a mix of **contributor** folders and **function** folders is recommended.

As long as we can pull site content from one folder and include it in a page stored in another folder, content contributors don't need access to pages that include much, if any, presentation logic. In other words, a *portal* page that includes content from multiple included pages doesn't need to be in a folder that's editable by any user group, as long as the *content* pages are accessible for editing.

Our portal page (`/ch9/portal/index.jsp`) includes the file `menu.jsp` to display our menu content. The menu file is displayed on nearly every page of the site, and in turn aggregates content from two separate files: `/it/menu.jsp` and `/hr/menu.jsp`. Thus, in order for an HR user to update HR content on every page of the site, the administrator can give the user access to the file `/hr/menu.jsp` include while restricting access to the portal page. IT users on the other hand can make changes to the exact same portal page by editing the `/it/menu.jsp` include.

With these ideas in mind, here's a suggestion for the folders to include in the root of a dynamic site that requires more than one user group and protects complex site code (I've left out folders that aren't important for learning about SSI or are automatically generated by Dreamweaver MX):

- `/admin`: Contains administrative interfaces. Pages in this folder will serve as entry points for content contributors to update their content (where they can choose to edit either their menu or content area), but these pages are not editable by users. They should only be editable by Dreamweaver developers

- `/hr`: Contains HR department content and menu items; the contents of this folder should be directly editable by HR users as well as developers, and are included in other site pages via `<jsp:include>` tags

- `/it`: Contains IT department content and menu items; the contents of this folder should be directly editable by IT users as well as developers, and are included in other site pages via `<jsp:include>` tags

- `/portal`: Contains pages aggregated from the separate content pages. Also contains sensitive JSP code that would cause site errors if tampered with. This should only be editable by Dreamweaver developers

While the content of the `/hr` and `/it` folders can appear on nearly every page of the site, content contributors do not need access to sensitive folders in order to keep the site current. The actual site folder structure is shown here:

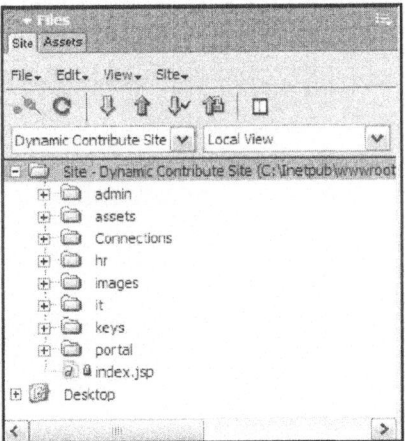

A dynamic site optimized for administration with Contribute can contain many folders.

Now we've seen what our entire site looks like, in the next section we'll look at how we can use Contribute to allow users to update our content without endangering our server-side code.

Configuring the Site for Contribute

Each of the include files discussed in the previous section are strong candidates for editing with Contribute because they contain no dynamic features, just plain HTML. Accidentally changing their content won't wreck the site's structure or generate errors on the page.

In this section, we'll first examine the completed HR admin page, and then we'll build the IT admin page from scratch and create a new Contribute user group for it.

An HR Administration Example

As you've seen, Contribute allows you to set folder permissions for different groups. A Contribute content editor can then navigate to the appropriate folder with Contribute's *Choose File on Website* dialog box in order to make changes. Although this is a great feature, if you use it for include files, you're making two dubious assumptions: first, you assume that your users understand or care about the concept of include files; second, you assume that you will always remember to give your include files intuitive, user-friendly names. It's much better to supplement standard Contribute dialog boxes with a visual method of opening SSI pages on the site.

Note: You will need to change this connection key in Dreamweaver to reflect your network configuration. The server on my home network is named irrawaddy, so my connection string is http://irrawaddy.mshome. net/ch9/.

Let's launch Contribute and then choose *Edit > My Connections*. When the *My Connections* dialog box opens, click *Import*. Browse to `/ch9/keys/` and double-click `DynamicContributeSite-HRUsers`. Provide a name and e-mail address, and then type the following password: `px44b3`.

Contribute will now open the administration homepage of the HR department. Note that HR users do not have permission to edit the page – this page simply helps the user navigate to the included files without having to understand the site structure. The page includes a key at the bottom to show the meaning of the colored squares: clicking on the blue square (the top one) opens the content page, and clicking on the orange square (the bottom one) opens the menu/announcements page.

In the HR Admin example, the user's homepage consists of an image map with links to editable pages. Users may find it easier to understand a visual metaphor for the site structure rather than learning the structure itself.

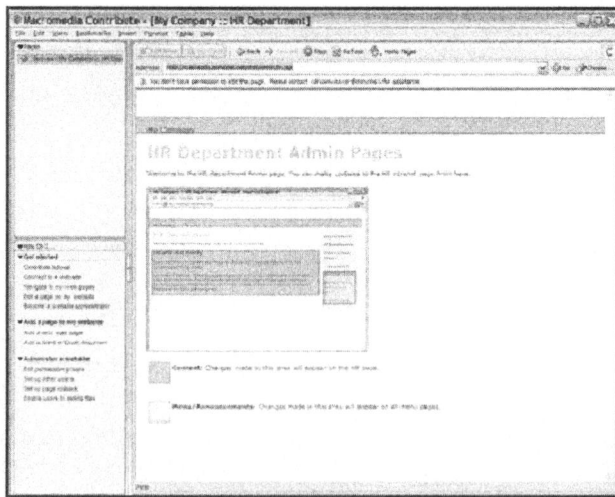

To test our application, click on the orange square. Contribute will open the page `/ch9/hr/menu.jsp`. Click the *Edit Page* button and change the second line of text from this:

```
Bonuses out next week!
```

to this:

```
Bonuses postponed.
```

Disregard the effect on company morale and click *Publish*. Contribute notifies you that the changes have been published. To test the changes, browse to any page of the site to see that, sadly enough, the bonuses have been postponed.

Let's build the IT Admin page from scratch.

Building the IT Admin Pages

Open the file `/ch9/admin/it.jsp` in Dreamweaver MX. As you can see, this file is simply a bare-bones page that we'll develop into the Contribute homepage for IT users.

Creating the Page Image

First, we will create the image that will become your users' visual reference.

- Open a web browser and navigate to our IT department page. The URL will be something like *http://localhost/ch9/portal/it.jsp*

- Take a screenshot of the page. If you're using Windows, you can take a screenshot by pressing *Alt-Print Screen*. If you're using a Mac, you can take a screenshot by pressing *Shift-Apple-3*

- Launch Fireworks MX (or another image editor of your choice), then paste the screenshot into Fireworks

- Now change the size of the image to something that fits comfortably on a web page (in Fireworks MX, choose *Modify > Canvas > Image Size*). I've changed my image size to 400 x 300 pixels, which is appropriate if your users are likely to be using a resolution such as 800 x 600

- Next we need to draw a box of some kind around the *IT Announcements* portion of the page and the content area of the page. We're not going to go into explicit details here, as instructions for doing this in different graphics packages can differ wildly. I used two solid rectangles, reducing the opacity of each so that the content below them is visible

Your image should now look something like this:

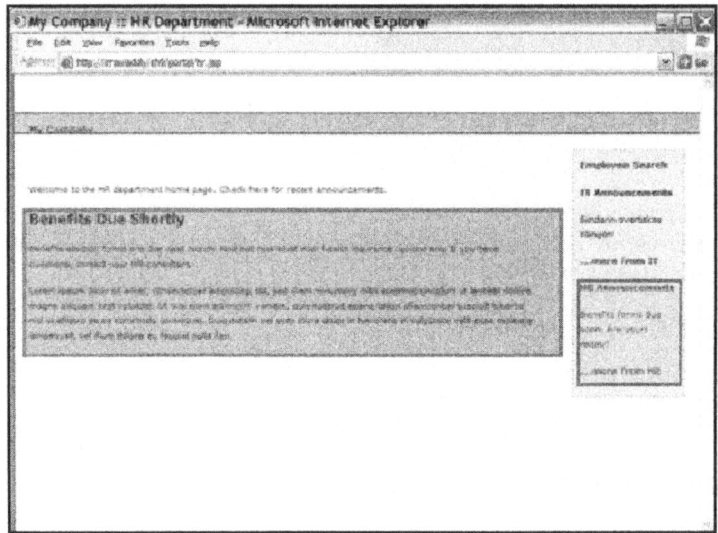

The image map for IT department users should point out both the content and announcement sections.

Now all we have left to do is export the image as a GIF to the images folder of your site. I named my image `it_home_page.gif` (you can find this in the code download for this chapter, available from *http://www.glasshaus.com*).

Building the Image Map

Next, we'll turn our image into an image map, so that your users can easily navigate to the content section they want to edit.

- Open the file `/ch9/admin/it.jsp` in Dreamweaver (or your HTML editor of choice)

- In the content `<div>` of the page, insert the image we just saved. This image will become the image map that your users click to edit pages. We've already drawn boxes over the portions of the screen that your users may edit; all that's left is to add the hotspots to the image

- Select the image and draw a hotspot over the blue rectangle. Link the hotspot to the URL `../it/content.jsp` (in Dreamweaver, select the *Rectangular Hotspot* tool in the *Property Inspector*)

- Draw another rectangular hotspot over the orange bow and link the hotspot to `../it/menu.jsp`

- Add explanatory text to the content `<div>` of your page. I've added a small key explaining the meaning of the colors

Of course, you're not required to use an HTML editor to build an image map. If you want to hand code the map, type the following lines after your `<img>` element:

```
<map name="Map">
  <area shape="rect" coords="7,101,312,180" href="../it/content.jsp">
  <area shape="rect" coords="322,91,378,152" href="../it/menu.jsp">
</map>
```

Our IT admin page should now look like this:

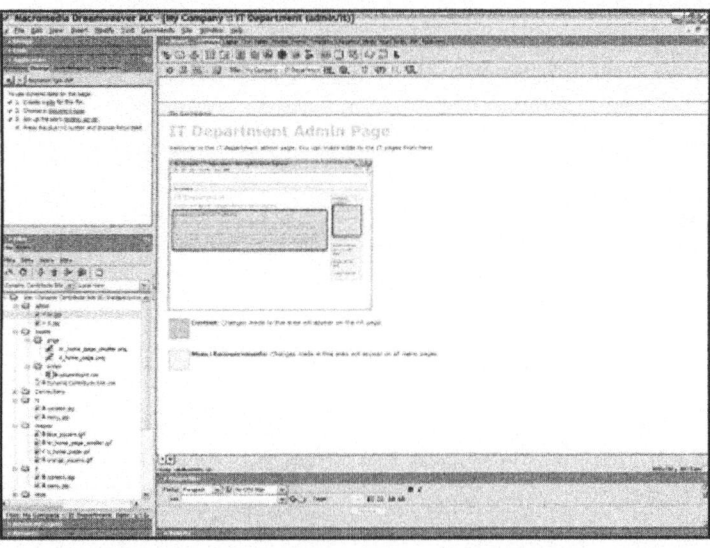

The IT admin page, with hotspots and explanatory text.

Now all that's left to do here is to save your page and test it in a browser. When you click the rectangles in the image of the page, your IT content pages should open.

Configuring the Contribute Permission Group

Now that you've created the image map, all that's left is to create a new Contribute user group, members of which will have permission to edit IT content. We also need to generate the site connection key. We'll move through these steps quickly, since you should be familiar with configuring sites for Contribute by now.

- In the site panel in Dreamweaver MX, choose *Site > Edit Sites*. The *Edit Sites* dialog box opens

- Choose the *Dynamic Contribute Site* and click *Edit*. The *Site Definition* dialog box opens. Click the *Advanced* tab

- In the *Category* list, click *Contribute* and then check *Administer Website* (if you imported the site definitions at the beginning of this chapter, the site will already be configured to work with Contribute). Provide the administrator password: jn5d6

- You should see two groups in the *Permission Group* panel: *Administrator* and *HR Users*. Click *New* to add a new group

8

- In the *Permission Group Name* dialog box, type *IT Users* and click *OK*. Click *Edit Group* to open the *Permission Group* dialog box

- In the general category, browse to the folder `/ch9/admin/it.jsp` and select it as your group homepage. The full address of your homepage will vary based on your configuration. For example, my server is named `irrawaddy` so my homepage is *http://irrawaddy.mshome.net/ch9/admin/it.jsp*

- In the *Folder/File Access* category, choose *Only allow editing within these folders*. Click *Add Folder*, and then double-click the `it` folder. Click *Select "it"*. This is the only folder IT users should have permission to edit

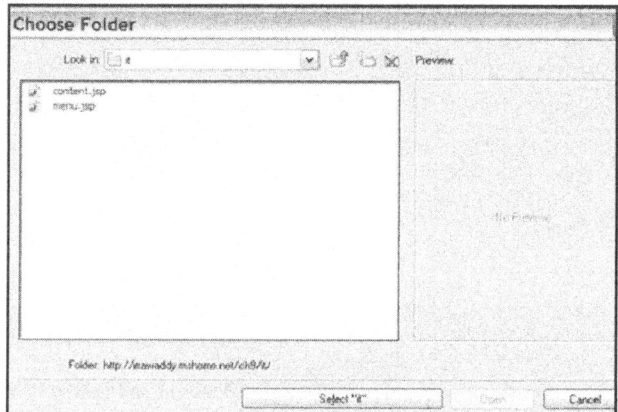

IT users should only have access to the it folder, as shown in the Choose Folder dialog of Contribute.

- Back in the *Permission Group* dialog box, in the *Editing* category choose *Only allow text editing and formatting*

- In the *Styles and Fonts* category, uncheck *Allow users to apply fonts and sizes*

- In the *New Pages* category, uncheck all options; in this case we do not wish to allow users to create new pages. Now click *OK*

When you have returned to the *Administer Website* dialog box, click *Send Connection Key* to open the Export Wizard:

- Choose *Yes* to export our connection settings and then click *Next*

- Choose the *IT Users* group to export and then click *Next*

- In the *Connection Key Information* screen, choose *Save to Local Machine*. Enter a password that we will give to your users: `ac743d`

- Click *Done* and save the key in the folder `/ch9/keys` folder. The default name, `DynamicContributeSite-ITUsers.stc`, is fine

Testing the Site

Now let's test our site in Contribute. Remember that when testing the site, we should try to put ourselves in the mindset of the user rather than the developer. It's worth getting a couple of non-techie friends in to test the site too, to see how usable it is to them.

Ideally, you should test the IT connection key on another machine than the one on which you tested the HR connection key, since the IT connection key will attempt to overwrite your original HR connection settings when you import it into Contribute.

- Double-click the `DynamicContributeSite-ITUsers.stc` file. Contribute will launch and open the *Import Connection Key* dialog box. If you already have Contribute open, simply import the key via the *My Connections* dialog. (See *Chapter 2* for more information on importing connection keys)

- Enter a name and e-mail address. Provide the connection key password (`ac743d`) and click *OK*. The user's homepage loads inside the Contribute browser

- Click the orange menu box in the page image map. The `/it/menu.jsp` page should load in the Contribute browser

- Click *Edit Page*. Note the editing information: *You only have permission to edit text on this page*

- Add new content to the page, and then click *Publish*. Contribute will save the changes to your web site

- If you'd like to view the change, log in to the site and view any page containing the site-wide menu. You should see the new message in the site's announcements/menu bar. It's as simple as that!

What You Can't Do with Contribute

In this chapter, you've learned how to structure your site and your pages in order to allow users to change the content of dynamic pages without breaking any dynamic code. You should be aware, however, of two important limitations of editing dynamic sites with Contribute:

- **You cannot use Contribute to add, edit, or delete information stored in your database:** Many organizations build content management systems that store text in a database to be served via HTML. Typically, the database text is updated via an HTML form interface. Contribute cannot take the place of a content management frontend that alters content stored in a database

- **You cannot use Contribute to edit static text on certain complex dynamic pages:** Many developers dynamically assemble an entire page based on user authorization. For example, an HR administrator might encounter different navigation options to an IT administrator, even though both users go to the same page. If the sections of your page are assembled dynamically based on user roles, Contribute may generate script errors and be unable to make updates. There's no hard and fast rule that governs when you can or cannot use Contribute on a dynamic site: Contribute doesn't have any problems opening and editing static text on a page with a simple database query, but it can choke on pages that depend on variables to assemble their layout. It's a good idea to back up your site and, as a Contribute administrator, experiment with different dynamic options. Your safest bet will always be to separate static text into include files, as discussed in this chapter

Dealing with Dynamic Sites

8

Summary

Take a moment to consider the power that the code-sharing model you've learned about in this chapter gives us. With server-side includes and Macromedia Contribute, an IT User on computer A can make changes to a list of announcements within a menu *at the same time* as an HR User on computer B makes changes *to the very same menu* – each with no danger of overwriting the other's work. Those changes will be reflected instantly, whether it's on five web pages or five hundred. This code-sharing model therefore provides a very useful alternative to templates.

In this chapter, you've learned:

- **How to assess templates versus server-side includes:** Each solution has its own strengths and weaknesses. Templates offer total control over code at the cost of locking you into a single development environment (Dreamweaver), while server-side includes offer instant site-wide propagation with the cost of adopting an application server

- **How to structure a dynamic site to be Contribute-ready:** As with all Contribute sites, planning your site structure and separating sensitive content wisely is key to a successful project

- **How to help your users work with the include model visually:** There's simply no need to force your users to learn the structure of the server-side includes on your site; instead, you can assist them visually by building image maps and navigation pages to the sections of the site they have permission to edit

Index

A Guide to the Index

The index is arranged in word-by-word order with preceding symbols ignored (so New York would appear before Newark and the <title> element among the 't's). Acronyms have been preferred to their expansions as main entries, being easier to recall or to work out.

As readers are likely to know, Contribute and Dreamweaver are products of Macromedia Corporation. For brevity, both names are frequently used without referring to the Corporation and the latter is sometimes abbreviated as DW or DWMX. Comments specifically about the index would be welcome at *indexers@glasshaus.com*

E

X

Z

Notes

Notes

Also from glasshaus:

Also from glasshaus:

Dreamweaver MX:
Advanced PHP Web Development

**Gareth Downes-Powell,
Tim Green, Allan Kent,
Bruno Mairlot, George McLachlan,
Dan Radigan**

1-904151-19-1

US: $39.99
C : $61.99
UK: £28.99

This book is the follow-up to "Dreamweaver MX: PHP Web Development" - the book described as "the VERY best book I have ever seen dealing with databases and web programming" by Matt Brown, Macromedia's Dreamweaver and Contribute Community Manager.

But you don't need to have read that book; any experience of developing PHP sites with Dreamweaver MX or UltraDev is a great starting point. This book takes your PHP sites beyond ther basic functions provided by server behaviors. It teaches you PHP, from the syntax to full applications, from the point of view of a Dreamweaver user.

Two practical case studies are built up: an on-line training log and a complete content management system.

Also from glasshaus:

glasshaus

web professional to web professional

Dynamic Dreamweaver MX

Rob Turnbull, Bob Regan, Omar Elbaga, Paul Boon, Rachel Andrew

1-904151-10-8

US: $29.99
C : $46.99
UK: £21.99

July 2002

This book gets you up to speed on using Macromedia Dreamweaver MX, the new version of Macromedia's premier visual web site design tool, to produce dynamic, creative, visually stunning sites that comply with web standards and accessibility guidelines. It gets straight to the heart of the matter so you spend less time reading, and more time building your site.

- **Rachel Andrew** is a member of the Web Standards Project's Dreamweaver Task Force, responsible for improving Dreamweaver's standards compliance and accessibility

- **Omar Elbaga** started out as a fine artist and moved to computer graphic arts. He is also a member of Team Macromedia

- **Alan Foley** is an Assistant Professor of Instructional Technology who teaches and consults on web accessibility and usability issues

- **Bob Regan** is the Senior Product Manager for Accessibility at Macromedia

- **Rob Turnbull** is also a member of Team Macromedia